FRANCIS

XVI ORDINARY GENERA
OF THE SYNOD OF BISHOPS

# FOR A SYNODAL CHURCH: COMMUNION, PARTICIPATION, MISSION

## Final Document

*All documents are published thanks to the generosity of the supporters of the Catholic Truth Society*

CATHOLIC TRUTH SOCIETY
PUBLISHERS TO THE HOLY SEE

*Cover image: Pope Francis attends the Second Session of the 16th Ordinary General Assembly of the Synod of Bishops at the Paul VI audience hall on 2nd October 2024 in The Vatican. Photo by Andreas Solaro/AFP via Getty Images.*

*This edition first published 2025 by The Incorporated Catholic Truth Society 42-46 Harleyford Road London SE11 5AY.*



*ISBN 978 1 78469 644 3*

# CONTENTS

# ABBREVIATIONS

| | |
|---|---|
| AA | VATICAN COUNCIL II, Decr. *Apostolicam Actuositatem* (18 November 1965) |
| AG | VATICAN COUNCIL II, Decr. *Ad Gentes* (7 December 1965) |
| DD | FRANCIS, Ap. Exhort. *Amoris Lætitia* (19 March 2022) |
| CCC | *Catechism of the Catholic Church* |
| CCEO | *Codex Canonum Ecclesiarum Orientalium* (18 October 1990) |
| CD | VATICAN COUNCIL II, Decr. *Christus Dominus* (28 October 1965) |
| CIC | *Codex Iuris Canonici* (25 January 1983) |
| CV | BENEDICT XVI, Enc. Lett. *Caritas in Veritate* (29 June 2009) |
| DCS | GENERAL SECRETARIAT OF THE SYNOD, *Working Document for the Continental Stage* (27 October 2022) |
| DD | FRANCIS, Ap. Lett. *Desiderio Desideravi* (29 June 2022) |
| DN | FRANCIS, Enc. Lett. *Dilexit Nos* (24 October 2024) |
| DV | VATICAN COUNCIL II, Dogm. Const. *Dei Verbum* (18 November 1965) |
| EC | FRANCIS, Ap. Const. *Episcopalis Communio* (15 September 2018) |
| EG | FRANCIS, Ap. Exhort. *Evangelii Gaudium* (24 November 2013) |

| | |
|---|---|
| EN | S. PAUL VI, Ap. Exhort. *Evangelii Nuntiandi* (8 December 1975) |
| FT | FRANCIS, Enc. Lett. *Fratelli Tutti* (3 October 2020) |
| GS | VATICAN COUNCIL II, Past. Const. *Gaudium et Spes* (7 December 1965) |
| ITC | INTERNATIONAL THEOLOGICAL COMMISSION, *Synodality in the Life and Mission of the Church* (2 March 2018) |
| LG | VATICAN COUNCIL II, Dogm. Const. *Lumen Gentium* (21 November 1964) |
| LS | FRANCIS, Enc. Lett. *Laudato Si'* (24 May 2015) |
| MC | S. PAUL VI, Ap. Exhort. *Marialis Cultus* (2 February 1974) |
| NMI | S. JOHN PAUL II, Ap. Lett. *Novo Millennio Ineunte* (6 January 2001) |
| PE | FRANCIS, Ap. Const. *Prædicate Evangelium* (19 March 2022) |
| SC | VATICAN COUNCIL II, Const. *Sacrosanctum Concilium* (4 December 1963) |
| SRS | S. JOHN PAUL II, Enc. Lett *Sollicitudo Rei Socialis* (30 December 1987) |
| UR | VATICAN COUNCIL II, Decr. *Unitatis Redintegratio* (21 November 1964) |
| UUS | S. JOHN PAUL II, Enc. Lett. *Ut Unum Sint* (25 May 1995) |

# ACCOMPANYING NOTE BY THE HOLY FATHER FRANCIS

In the various moments of the journey of the Synod that I launched in October 2021, we have been listening to what the Holy Spirit is saying to the Churches at this time.

The *Final Document* of the XVI Ordinary General Assembly of the Synod of Bishops gathers the fruits of a journey marked by listening to the People of God and by the discernment of Pastors. The whole Church, allowing itself to be enlightened by the Holy Spirit, was called to review its own experience and identify the steps to be taken to live communion, realise participation and promote the mission that Jesus Christ entrusted to the Church. The synodal journey began in the local Churches and then proceeded through the national and continental phases, leading to the celebration of the Assembly of the Synod of Bishops in the two sessions of October 2023 and October 2024. Now, the journey continues in the local Churches and their groupings, treasuring the *Final Document* that was voted on and approved by the Assembly in all its parts on 26 October. I, too, approved it and, signing it, ordered its publication, joining the 'we' of the Assembly, which, through the *Final Document*, addresses the holy faithful People of God.

Acknowledging the value of the synodal journey undertaken, I now hand over to the whole Church all that is contained in the *Final Document* restoring to the Church what has matured over these years through listening and discernment and as an authoritative orientation for the Church's life and mission.

The *Final Document* is part of the ordinary Magisterium of the Successor of Peter (cf. EC 18 § 1; CCC 892), and as such, I ask that it be welcomed and received. It represents a form of exercise of the authentic teaching of the Bishop of Rome that has some novel features but which, in fact, corresponds to what I had the opportunity to point out on 17 October 2015, when I affirmed that synodality is the appropriate interpretative framework for understanding hierarchical ministry.

In approving the *Final Document* on 26 October, I said that it 'is not strictly normative' and that 'its application will need various mediations'. This does not mean that it does not commit the Churches from now on to make choices consistent with what is stated in it. The local Churches and groupings of Churches are now called upon to implement, in their different contexts, the authoritative proposals contained in the *Document* through the processes of discernment and decision-making provided for by law and by the *Document* itself. In my *Final Greeting*, I also added that 'time is needed in order to arrive at decisions that involve the whole Church'. This is particularly true for the topics entrusted to the ten study groups, to which others may be added as necessary decisions are made. The conclusion of the XVI Ordinary General Assembly of the Synod of Bishops does not put an end to the synodal process.

I take up here with conviction what I indicated at the end of the complex and co-ordinated synodal path that led to the promulgation of *Amoris lætitia* (19 March 2016): 'Not all discussions of doctrinal, moral or pastoral issues need to be settled by interventions of the magisterium. Unity of teaching and practice is certainly necessary in the Church, but this does not preclude various ways of interpreting some aspects of that teaching or drawing certain consequences from it. This will always be the case as the Spirit guides us towards the entire truth (cf. Jn 16:13), until he leads us fully into the mystery of Christ and enables us to see all things as he does. Each country or region, moreover, can seek solutions better suited to its culture and sensitive to its traditions and local needs.' (AL 3).

The *Final Document* contains proposals that, in the light of its basic orientations, can already now be implemented in the local Churches and groupings of Churches, taking into account different contexts, what has already been done, and what remains to be done so that the style proper to the missionary synodal Church can be ever-better learned and developed.

In many cases, it is a matter of effectively implementing what is already provided for in existing law, both Latin and Eastern. In other cases, it will be possible to proceed, through a synodal discernment and within the framework of the possibilities outlined in the *Final Document*, to the creative activation of new forms of ministeriality and missionary action, experimenting and testing or verifying these experiences. In the report envisaged for the *ad limina* visit, each bishop will take care to report what choices have been made in the local Church entrusted to him in relation to the indications in the *Final Document*, what difficulties have arisen, and what fruits have resulted.

The task of accompanying the 'implementation phase' of the synodal path, on the basis of the guidelines offered by the *Final Document*, is entrusted to the General Secretariat of the Synod together with the Dicasteries of the Roman Curia (cf. EC 19-21).

The synodal path of the Catholic Church, also animated by the desire to continue the journey towards the full and visible unity of Christians, 'needs shared words to be accompanied by actions' (*Final Greeting*, 26 October 2024). May the Holy Spirit, gift of the Risen Lord, sustain and guide the whole Church on this journey. May the Holy Spirit, who is harmony, continue to rejuvenate the Church with the power of the Gospel, renew her and lead her to perfect union with her Bridegroom (cf. LG 4). For the Spirit and the Bride say to the Lord Jesus: 'Come' (cf. Rev 22:17).

*Vatican, 24 November 2024*
*Solemnity of Our Lord Jesus Christ King of the Universe*

Franciscus

# INTRODUCTION[1]

*Jesus came and stood among them and said, "Peace be with you." After he said this, he showed them his hands and his side. Then the disciples rejoiced when they saw the Lord (Jn 20:19-20).*

1. Every new step in the life of the Church is a return to the source. It is a renewed experience of the disciples' encounter with the Risen One in the Upper Room on Easter evening. Like them, during this synodal Assembly, we, too, felt enfolded in His mercy and drawn to His beauty. We felt His presence in our midst as we lived conversation in the Spirit and listened to one another: the presence of He who, in bestowing the Holy Spirit, continues to build among His people a unity that establishes harmony amidst differences.

2. Contemplating the Risen One, we recall that we "have been baptised [...] into his death" (*Rom* 6:3). We have seen the mark of His wounds transfigured by a new life, yet engraved forever in His humanity. These are wounds that continue to bleed in the bodies of many brothers and sisters, including as a result of our own actions. Looking upon the Lord does not distance us from the tragedies of history. Instead, it opens our eyes to the suffering of those around us, and we are pierced: the faces of war-stricken terrorised children, weeping mothers, the shattered dreams of so many young people, refugees who face terrible journeys, the victims of climate change and social injustice. Their sufferings have resounded among us not only via the media but also through the voices of many amongst us in our Assembly whose families and peoples have been directly involved in these tragic events. In the days during which we have been gathered, wars have

[1] The *Final Document* of the XVI Ordinary General Assembly of the Synod of Bishops was approved during the 17th General Congregation, on 26 October 2024, with the favourable vote of more than two-thirds of the Assembly Members present at the voting. The results of the vote are available at www.vatican.va. The official version of the text is in Italian. In preparation for publication, editorial changes were made to ensure linguistic correctness and fluency, as well as the accuracy of quotations.

continued to cause death and destruction, a desire for revenge and a loss of conscience. We join Pope Francis in his repeated appeals for peace, condemning the logic of violence, hatred and revenge and committing ourselves to promoting the logic of dialogue, fellowship and reconciliation. Genuine and lasting peace is possible, and together we can build it. "The joys and hopes and the sorrows and anxieties of people today, especially of those who are poor and afflicted" (GS 1) have been once again the joys and sorrows of all of us, Christ's disciples.

3. Since 2021, when the Holy Father embarked the Church upon this synodal journey, we have been discovering its richness and fruitfulness more and more. We began by listening, taking care to grasp in the many voices "what the Spirit is saying to the Churches" (*Rev* 2:7). The journey began with the vast consultation of the People of God in our dioceses and eparchies and continued with the national and continental stages. This cycle of dialogue has been continually reinvigorated by the General Secretariat for the Synod of Bishops through the Synthesis Reports and Working Documents. The celebration of the XVI Ordinary General Assembly of the Synod of Bishops in its two sessions has permitted us today to present to the Holy Father and to all the Churches this witness to what we have experienced and the fruit of our discernment for a renewed missionary impulse. During each stage, the journey was characterised by the wisdom of the "sense of faith" (*sensus fidei*) of the People of God. Step by step, we came to understand that at the heart of the *Synod 2021-2024. For a Synodal Church: Communion, Participation, Mission* there is a call to joy and to the renewal of the Church in following the Lord, in committing to service of His mission, and in searching for ways to be faithful.

4. This call is based upon a shared baptismal identity. It is rooted in the diversity of contexts in which the Church is present and finds unity in the one Father, one Lord, and one Spirit. It challenges all the Baptised, without exception: "The whole People of God is an agent of the proclamation of the Gospel.

Every baptised person is called to be a protagonist of mission since we are all missionary disciples" (ITC 53). For this reason, the synodal journey directs us towards a full and visible unity of Christians, as the presence of delegates of other Christian traditions testifies. Unity ferments within the holy Church of God, prophetically so, for the entire world.

5. Rooted in the Tradition of the Church, the entire synodal journey took place in the light of the conciliar Magisterium. The Second Vatican Council was indeed like a seed thrown onto the field of the world and the Church. The daily life of believers, the experience of the Churches in every people and culture, the many testimonies of holiness, and the reflection of theologians represented the soil upon which it has taken root and grown. The *Synod 2021-2024* continues to draw upon the energy of that seed and develop its potential, putting into practice what the Council taught about the Church as Mystery and Church as People of God, called to holiness through a continual conversion that comes from listening to the Gospel. In this sense, the synodal journey constitutes a further act of reception of the Council, thus deepening its inspiration and reinvigorating its prophetic force for today's world.

6. We cannot deny that we have faced fatigue, resistance to change and the temptation to let our own ideas prevail over listening to the Gospel and the practice of discernment. Yet the mercy of God, our most loving Father, purifies our hearts, thus enabling us to continue along this journey. Acknowledging this, we began the Second Session of the Assembly with a penitential vigil, through which, feeling our shame, we asked forgiveness for our sins, and we lifted up our prayers for the victims of the evils of the world. We identified our sins: against peace, against Creation, against indigenous peoples, migrants, children, women, and those who are poor, in our failure to listen and to seek communion. We were brought to a renewed understanding, namely, that synodality requires repentance and conversion. In celebrating the sacrament of the mercy of God, we experience

unconditional love: the hardness of heart is conquered, and we open ourselves to communion. This is why we want to be a merciful Church, capable of sharing with everyone the forgiveness and reconciliation that come from God: the pure grace of which we are not masters but only witnesses.

7. We were able to witness to the first fruits of the synodal journey that began in 2021, the simplest and most precious of which mature in the life of families, parishes, movements, small Christian communities, schools and other movements. This is where the practice of conversation in the Spirit, community discernment, sharing of vocational gifts and co-responsibility in the mission is growing. The meeting of *Parish Priests for the Synod* (Sacrofano [Rome] 28 April – 2 May 2024) made it possible to listen closely to these rich experiences and to renew the journey. We are grateful and happy for the voices of many communities and of the faithful who ensure that the Church is experienced as a place of welcome, hope and joy.

8. The first Session of the Assembly has yielded other results. The Synthesis Report drew attention to key themes of great importance for the life of the Church. The Holy Father, at the end of an international consultation, entrusted these themes to Study Groups made up of pastors and experts from all continents, who were asked to work using a synodal methodology. The areas of the life and mission of the Church that they have already begun to study in depth are the following:

1. Some aspects of the relationship between the Eastern Catholic Churches and the Latin Church.
2. Listening to the cry of the poor and the earth.
3. The mission in the digital environment.
4. The revision of the *Ratio Fundamentalis Institutionis Sacerdotalis* in a missionary synodal perspective.
5. Some theological and canonical matters regarding specific ministerial forms.

6. The revision, in a synodal missionary perspective, of the documents touching on the relationship between Bishops, consecrated life, and ecclesial associations.

7. Some aspects of the person and ministry of the Bishop (in particular: criteria for selecting candidates to the episcopacy, the judicial function of the Bishops, the nature and structure of *ad limina Apostolorum* visits) from a missionary synodal perspective.

8. The role of Pontifical Representatives in a missionary synodal perspective.

9. Theological criteria and synodal methodologies for shared discernment of controversial doctrinal, pastoral and ethical issues.

10. The reception of the fruits of the ecumenical journey in the People of God.

Furthermore, in agreement with the Dicastery for Legislative Texts, a Canonical Commission has been established to work on innovations needed regarding ecclesial norms. In addition, discernment concerning the pastoral accompaniment of people in polygamous marriages has been entrusted to the Symposium of the Episcopal Conferences of Africa and Madagascar. The work of these groups and commissions has marked the beginning of the implementation stage, has enriched the work of the Second Session, and will assist the Holy Father in pastoral and governance decisions.

9. The synodal process does not conclude with the end of the current Assembly of the Synod of Bishops but also includes the implementation phase. As members of the Assembly and as synodal missionaries within the communities from which we come, we feel it is our responsibility to promote this process. The local Churches are asked to continue their daily journey with a synodal methodology of consultation and discernment, identifying concrete ways and formation pathways to bring

about a tangible synodal conversion in the various ecclesial contexts (parishes, Institutes of consecrated life and Societies of apostolic life, movements of the faithful, dioceses, Episcopal Conferences, groupings of Churches, etc.). Planning for an evaluation of the progress made in terms of synodality and the participation of all the Baptised in the life of the Church should also occur. We suggest to the Episcopal Conferences and Synods of the Churches *sui iuris* to allocate personnel and resources to accompany the pathway of growth as a synodal Church in mission and to maintain contact with the General Secretariat of the Synod (cf. EC 19 § 1 and 2). We ask the Secretariat to continue to watch over the synodal quality of the working method of the Study Groups.

10. This *Final Document*, offered to the Holy Father and to the Churches as the fruit of the XVI General Assembly of the Synod of Bishops, encapsulates all the steps taken so far. It brings together the important convergences that emerged during the First Session, the contributions that arrived from the Churches in the months between the First and Second Sessions, and what has matured, especially through conversation in the Spirit, during the Second Session.

11. The *Final Document* expresses awareness that the call to mission is, at the same time, the call to the conversion of each local Church and of the whole Church, in line with the Apostolic Exhortation *Evangelii Gaudium* (cf. EG 30). There are five parts to the text. The first, entitled *The Heart of Synodality*, outlines the theological and spiritual foundations that enlighten and nourish what is to come. It restates the shared understanding of synodality that emerged in the First Session and develops its spiritual and prophetic perspectives. The conversion of the emotions, images and thoughts inhabiting our hearts proceeds together with the conversion of pastoral and missionary action. The second part, entitled *On the Boat, Together*, is dedicated to the conversion of the relationships that are formed in the intertwining of vocations, charisms and ministries, building the

Christian community and shaping mission. The third part, *"Cast the Net,"* identifies three practices that are intimately connected: ecclesial discernment, decision-making processes, and a culture of transparency, accountability and evaluation. With respect to these, we are also asked to initiate pathways of 'missionary transformation', for which a renewal of participatory bodies is urgently needed. The fourth part, under the title *An Abundant Catch*, outlines how we can cultivate new forms of the exchange of gifts and renew the intertwining of the bonds that unite us in the Church at a time when the experience of being rooted in a place is changing profoundly. This is followed by a fifth part, *"So I Send You,"* which enables us to look at a particular step we need to take: caring for the formation of all, of the People of God, all as synodal missionaries.

12. The development of the *Final Document* is guided by the Gospel Resurrection narratives. The race to the tomb on Easter morning and the appearances of the Risen One in the Upper Room and on the lake shore inspired our discernment and enriched our dialogue. We invoked the Easter gift of the Holy Spirit, asking Him to teach us what we must do and show us the way forward together. With this document, the Assembly recognises and bears witness that synodality, a constitutive dimension of the Church, is already part of the experience of many of our communities. At the same time, it suggests pathways to follow, practices to implement and horizons to explore. The Holy Father, who convened the Church in Synod, will instruct the Churches, entrusted to the pastoral care of the Bishops, how to continue our journey supported by the hope that "does not disappoint us" (*Rom* 5:5).

# PART I - THE HEART OF SYNODALITY

## CALLED BY THE HOLY SPIRIT TO CONVERSION

*Early on the first day of the week, while it was still dark, Mary Magdalene came to the tomb and saw that the stone had been removed from the tomb. So she ran and went to Simon Peter and the other disciple, the one whom Jesus loved (Jn 20:1-2).*

13. We encounter three disciples on Easter Morning: Mary Magdalene, Simon Peter, and the disciple whom Jesus loved. Each of them is seeking the Lord in his or her own way; each has his or her own part to play in enabling the light of hope to dawn. Mary Magdalene is so driven by love that she is the first at the tomb. Alerted by her, Peter and the Beloved Disciple make their way to the tomb. The Beloved Disciple races to the tomb with all the strength of youth. He looks intently; he is the first to understand, yet he lets Peter go first, he who is the elder, entrusted with the responsibility of leading. Peter, weighed down by his renunciation of the Lord, has an appointment with mercy, the mercy which he will minister in the Church. Mary remains in the garden. She hears herself called by name. She recognises the Lord. He commissions her to proclaim his Resurrection to the community of disciples. For this reason, the Church recognises her as Apostle of the Apostles. Their dependence on one another embodies the heart of synodality.

14. The Church exists to bear witness in the world to the most decisive moment in history: the Resurrection of Jesus. The Risen Christ brings peace to the world and gives us the gift of His Spirit. The living Christ is the source of true freedom, the foundation for a hope that does not disappoint, the revelation

of the true face of God and humanity's ultimate destiny. The Gospels tell us that in order to enter into Easter faith and become witnesses to it, it is necessary to acknowledge our own inner emptiness, the darkness of fear, doubt and sin. Yet those who, in the midst of darkness, find the courage to set out as searchers discover that they themselves are the ones being sought. They are being called by name, offered forgiveness, and, in turn, sent out to their brothers and sisters together.

## THE CHURCH AS THE PEOPLE OF GOD, SACRAMENT OF UNITY

15. The identity of the People of God flows from Baptism in the name of the Father and of the Son and of the Holy Spirit. This identity is lived out as a call to holiness and a sending out in mission, inviting all peoples to accept the gift of salvation (cf. *Mt* 28:18-19). The missionary synodal Church springs from Baptism, in which Christ clothes us with Himself (cf. *Gal* 3:27) and enables us to be reborn of the Spirit (cf. *Jn* 3:5-6) as children of God. The whole of Christian existence has its source and horizon in the mystery of the Trinity, which brings forth in us the dynamism of faith, hope and love.

16. "It has pleased God, however, to sanctify and save men and women not individually and without regard for what binds them together, but to set them up as a people who would acknowledge Him in truth and serve Him in holiness" (LG 9). The Eucharist, the source of communion and unity, continually nourishes the People of God on their journey towards the Kingdom: "Because there is one bread, we who are many are one body, for we all partake of the one bread." (*1 Cor* 10:17). The Church, nourished by the Sacrament of the Body and Blood of the Lord, is constituted as His Body (cf. LG 7): "you are the body of Christ and individually members of it." (*1 Cor* 12:27). Enlivened by grace, the Church is a temple of the Holy Spirit (cf. LG 17); the Spirit animates and builds it, making us all living stones of a spiritual edifice (cf. *1 Pet* 2:5; LG 6).

17. Gathered from every tribe, language, people and nation and living in different contexts and cultures, the synodal process gave us the "spiritual taste" (EG 268) of what it means to be the People of God. The People of God is never the simple sum of the Baptised but the communitarian and historical subject of synodality and mission still on pilgrimage through time and already in communion with the Church in heaven. Within the plurality of contexts where the local Churches are rooted, the People of God proclaim and bear witness to the Good News of salvation. Being in the world and for the world, they walk together with all the peoples of the earth, in dialogue with their religions and their cultures, recognising in them the seeds of the Word, journeying towards the Kingdom. Incorporated into the People of God by faith and Baptism, we are sustained and accompanied by the Virgin Mary, "a sign of sure hope and comfort" (LG 68), by the Apostles, by those who bore witness to their faith to the point of giving their lives, and by the saints of every time and place.

18. In the holy People of God, which is the Church, the communion of the faithful (*communio fidelium*) is at the same time the communion of the Churches (*communio Ecclesiarum*), which is manifested in the communion of Bishops (*communio Episcoporum*) by reason of the very ancient principle that "the Church is in the Bishop and the Bishop is in the Church" (St Cyprian, *Epistle* 66, 8). The Lord placed the Apostle Peter (cf. *Mt* 16:18) and his successors at the service of this manifold communion. By virtue of the Petrine ministry, the Bishop of Rome is "the perpetual and visible principle and foundation" (LG 23) of the Church's unity.

19. "God's heart has a special place for the poor" (EG 197), the marginalised and the excluded. Therefore, they are at the heart of the Church. The whole Christian community is called to recognise in those made poor the face and flesh of Christ, who, though He was rich, became poor for us so that we might become rich through His poverty (cf. *2 Cor* 8:9). The preferential

option for the poor is implicit in Christological faith. The direct knowledge of the suffering Christ (cf. EG 198) possessed by those who are poor makes them heralds of salvation received as a gift and witnesses to the joy of the Gospel. The Church is called to be poor with those who are poor, who often constitute the majority of the faithful, to listen to them, learning together how to recognise the charisms they receive from the Spirit. The Church also needs to learn to recognise them as agents of evangelisation.

20. "Christ is the light of the nations" (LG 1), and this light shines on the face of the Church, even when marked by the fragility of the human condition obscured by sin. The Church receives from Christ the gift and responsibility of being the effective leaven in bonds, relationships and the kinship of the human family (cf. AG 2-4), witnessing to the meaning and goal of its journey in the world (cf. GS 3 and 42). The Church assumes this responsibility today at a time dominated by a crisis of participation, that is, of people feeling that they are not participants or actors with a common destiny, as well as by an individualistic understanding of happiness and salvation. The Church's vocation and prophetic service (cf. LG 12) consist in witnessing to God's plan to unite all humanity to Himself in freedom and communion. The Church is "the kingdom of Christ already present in mystery" (LG 3) and "the seed and the beginning of the kingdom on earth" (LG 5). It, therefore, walks together with all humanity, strongly committed to justice and peace, human dignity and the common good. All this, while it "aspires after the completion of the kingdom" (LG 5) when God will be "all in all" (*1 Cor* 15:28).

## THE SACRAMENTAL ROOTS OF THE PEOPLE OF GOD

21. The synodal journey of the Church led us to rediscover the root of the varieties of charisms, vocations and ministries: "we were all baptised into one body [...] and we were all made to drink of one Spirit." (*1 Cor* 12:13). Baptism is the foundation of Christian life. This is because it introduces everyone to the greatest gift, which is to be children of God, that is, to share in

Jesus's relationship to the Father in the Spirit. There is nothing higher than this baptismal dignity, equally bestowed upon each person, through which we are invited to clothe ourselves with Christ and be grafted onto Him like branches of the one vine. The name "Christian", which we have the honour of being called, contains the grace that is the basis of our life and enables us to walk together as brothers and sisters.

22. Through Baptism, "the holy People of God has a share, too, in the prophetic role of Christ, when it renders Him a living witness, especially through a life of faith and charity" (LG 12). The anointing by the Holy Spirit received at Baptism (cf. *1 Jn* 2:20.27) enables all believers to possess an instinct for the truth of the Gospel. We refer to this as the *sensus fidei*. This consists in a certain connaturality with divine realities based on the fact that, in the Holy Spirit, the Baptised become "sharers [participants] in the divine nature" (DV 2). From this participation comes the aptitude to grasp intuitively what conforms to the truth of Revelation in the communion of the Church. This is the reason why the Church is certain that the holy People of God cannot err in matters of belief. They manifest this special property when they show universal agreement in matters of faith and morals (cf. LG 12). The exercise of the *sensus fidei* must not be confused with public opinion. It is always in conjunction with the discernment of pastors at the different levels of Church life, as the various interconnected phases of the synodal process demonstrated. The *sensus fidei* aims at reaching a consensus of the faithful (*consensus fidelium*), which constitutes "a sure criterion for determining whether a particular doctrine or practice belongs to the apostolic faith" (ITC, Sensus fidei *in the life of the Church*, 2014, 3).

23. All Christians participate in the *sensus fidei* through Baptism. Therefore, as well as constituting the basis of synodality, Baptism is also the foundation of ecumenism. "The journey of synodality undertaken by the Catholic Church is and must be ecumenical, just as the ecumenical journey is synodal" (Pope Francis, *Address to His Holiness Mar Awa III*, 19 November

2022). Ecumenism is, first and foremost, a matter of spiritual renewal. It demands processes of repentance and the healing of memories of past wounds and, where necessary, finding the courage to offer fraternal correction in a spirit of evangelical charity. The Assembly resounded with profound testimonies by Christians of different ecclesial traditions who share friendship and prayer, live together in community, are committed to serving those living in various forms of poverty, and care for our common home. In many regions of the world, there is, above all, the ecumenism of blood: Christians of different backgrounds who together give their lives for faith in Jesus Christ. The witness of their martyrdom is more eloquent than any word: unity comes from the Cross of the Lord.

24. Baptism is understood more fully when placed in the context of Christian Initiation, that is, the journey through which the Lord, through the ministry of the Church, introduces us to the Paschal faith and draws us into Trinitarian and ecclesial communion. This journey takes significantly various forms depending on the age at which it is undertaken, the different emphases proper to the Eastern and Western traditions, and the specificities of each local Church. Initiation brings each person into contact with a great variety of vocations and ecclesial ministries. These embody the merciful face of the Church who, like a mother, teaches her children to walk by walking alongside them. The Church listens to those in initiation, addressing their doubts and questions, and is enriched by the newness each person brings by means of his or her own history and culture. In the practice of this pastoral action, the Christian community experiences, often without being fully aware of it, the first form of synodality.

25. Within the journey of Christian Initiation, the Sacrament of Confirmation enriches the lives of believers with a special outpouring of the Spirit so that they become witnesses to faith. The Spirit with whom Jesus was filled (cf. *Lk* 4:1), who anointed Him and sent Him to proclaim the Gospel (cf. *Lk* 4:18), is the

same Spirit poured out on believers. This sanctifying anointing seals their belonging to God. For this reason, Confirmation, which renders the grace of Pentecost present in the lives of the baptised person and the community, is a valuable gift. It renews in us the miracle of a Church stirred up by the fire of mission, with the courage to go out onto the streets of the world with the ability to be understood by all peoples and cultures. All believers are called to contribute to this impetus, accepting the charisms that the Spirit distributes abundantly to each one and committing themselves to place these at the service of the Reign of God with humility and creative resourcefulness.

26. The celebration of the Eucharist, especially on Sundays, is the first and fundamental way the holy People of God gather and meet. "The unity of the Church is both signified and made a reality" (UR 2) by the celebration of the Eucharist. In the "full, conscious and active" (SC 14) participation of all the faithful, in the presence of different ministries and in the presidency of the Bishop or Priest, the Christian community is made visible, whereby a differentiated co-responsibility of all for mission is fulfilled. For this reason, the Church, the Body of Christ, learns from the Eucharist how to combine unity and plurality: the unity of the Church and the multiplicity of Eucharistic assemblies; unity of the sacramental mystery and variety of liturgical traditions; unity of celebration and plurality of vocations, charisms and ministries. The Eucharist, above all else, demonstrates that the harmony created by the Spirit is not uniformity and that every ecclesial gift is destined for the common good of all. Every celebration of the Eucharist is also an expression of the desire and call to a unity of all the Baptised not yet fully visible. Should celebrating the Sunday Eucharist not be possible despite the desire to do so, the community gathers around the celebration of the Word, where Christ is, in any case, present.

27. There is a close link between *synaxis* and *synodos*, between the Eucharistic assembly and the synodal assembly. In both cases, albeit in different forms, Jesus's promise to be present

where two or three are gathered in His name is fulfilled (cf. *Mt* 18:20). Synodal assemblies are events that celebrate the union of Christ with His Church through the action of the Spirit. It is the Spirit who ensures the unity of the ecclesial body of Christ in the Eucharistic assembly as well as in the synodal assembly. The liturgy is a listening to the Word of God and a response to His covenantal initiative. Similarly, the synodal assembly is a listening to this same Word, which resounds as much in the signs of the times as in the hearts of the faithful, and also a response of the assembly that is discerning God's will in order to put it into practice. Deepening the link between liturgy and synodality will help all Christian communities, in the diversity of their cultures and traditions, to adopt celebratory styles that make visible the face of a synodal Church. To this end, we call for the establishment of a specific Study Group which would be entrusted with reflection on how to make liturgical celebrations more an expression of synodality. It could also consider the topic of preaching within liturgical celebrations as well as the development of catechetical resources on synodality from a mystagogical perspective.

## MEANING AND DIMENSIONS OF SYNODALITY

28. The terms '*synodality*' and '*synodal*' derive from the ancient and constant ecclesial practice of meeting in synods. According to the traditions of the Eastern and Western Churches, the word 'synod' refers to institutions and events that assumed different forms over time, involving a plurality of agents and participants. This variety notwithstanding, what unites them is gathering together to dialogue, discern and decide. Owing to the experience of recent years, the meaning of these terms has come to be better understood, and what they represent is more vibrantly lived. They have become ever more deeply associated with the desire for a Church that is closer to people and more relational – a Church that is God's home and family. During the synodal journey, we have witnessed a fruitful convergence regarding the meaning of synodality that forms the basis of this

Document. Synodality is the walking together of Christians with Christ and towards God's Kingdom, in union with all humanity. Orientated towards mission, synodality involves gathering at all levels of the Church for mutual listening, dialogue and community discernment. It also involves reaching consensus as an expression of Christ rendering Himself present, He who is alive in the Spirit. Furthermore, it consists in reaching decisions according to differentiated co-responsibilities. Along these lines, we can understand better what it means to say that synodality is a constitutive dimension of the Church (cf. ITC 1). In simple and concise terms, synodality is a path of spiritual renewal and structural reform that enables the Church to be more participatory and missionary so that it can walk with every man and woman, radiating the light of Christ.

29. We see the features of a synodal, missionary and merciful Church shining in full light in the Virgin Mary, Mother of Christ, of the Church and of humanity. She is the form of the Church who listens, prays, meditates, dialogues, accompanies, discerns, decides and acts. From Her we learn the art of listening, attentiveness to God's will, obedience to God's Word and a readiness to hear the needs of those who are poor and to set out along the path. We also learn the love that reaches out to aid those in need and the song of praise that exults in the Spirit. For this reason, as St Paul VI said, "the action of the Church in the world can be likened to an extension of Mary's concern" (MC, 28).

30. Specifically, synodality designates three distinct aspects of the life of the Church:

a) in the first instance, it refers to "the particular style that qualifies the life and mission of the Church, expressing her nature as the People of God journeying together and gathering in assembly, summoned by the Lord Jesus in the power of the Holy Spirit to proclaim the Gospel. Synodality ought to be expressed in the Church's ordinary way of living and working. This *modus vivendi et operandi* works through the community listening to the Word and celebrating the Eucharist, the brotherhood of communion and the co-responsibility and participation of the whole People of God in its life and mission, on all levels and distinguishing between various ministries and roles" (ITC 70.a);

b) secondly, "(i)n a more specific sense, which is determined from a theological and canonical point of view, synodality denotes those structures and ecclesial processes in which the synodal nature of the Church is expressed at an institutional level, but analogously on various levels: local, regional and universal. These structures and processes are officially at the service of the Church, which must discover the way to move forward by listening to the Holy Spirit" (ITC 70.b);

c) thirdly, synodality designates "the programme of those synodal events in which the Church is called together by the competent authority in accordance with the specific procedures laid down by ecclesiastical discipline, involving the whole People of God in various ways on local, regional and universal levels, presided over by the Bishops in collegial communion with the Bishop of Rome, to discern the way forward and other particular questions, and to take particular decisions and directions with the aim of fulfilling its evangelising mission" (ITC 70.c).

31. In the context of the ecclesiology of the Council, with reference to the People of God, the concept of communion expresses the profound substance of the mystery and mission of the Church. This mystery has its source and summit in the celebration of the Eucharist, that is, in union with God the Trinity and in the unity among human persons realised in Christ through the Holy Spirit. Against this background, synodality "is the specific *modus vivendi et operandi* of the Church, the People of God, which reveals and gives substance to her being as communion when all her members journey together, gather in assembly and take an active part in her evangelising mission" (ITC 6).

32. Synodality is not an end in itself. Rather, it serves the mission that Christ entrusted to the Church in the Spirit. To evangelise is "the essential mission of the Church. It is [...] the grace and vocation proper to the Church, her deepest identity" (EN 14). By being close to all without distinction of persons, preaching and teaching, baptising, and celebrating the Eucharist and the Sacrament of Reconciliation, all the local Churches and the whole Church respond concretely to the Lord's command to proclaim the Gospel to all nations (cf. *Mt* 28:19-20; *Mk* 16:15-16). By appreciating all charisms and ministries, synodality enables the People of God to proclaim and witness to the Gospel to women and men of every place and time, making itself a "visible sacrament" (LG 9) of the fellowship and unity in Christ willed by God. Synodality and mission are intimately linked: mission illuminates synodality and synodality spurs to mission.

33. The authority of pastors "is a specific gift of the Spirit of Christ the Head for the upbuilding of the entire Body" (ITC 67). This gift is bound to the Sacrament of Orders, which configures pastors to Christ, Head, Shepherd and Servant, and places them at the service of the holy People of God in order to safeguard the apostolicity of the proclamation and to promote ecclesial communion at all levels. Synodality offers "the most appropriate interpretive framework for understanding the hierarchical ministry itself" (Francis, *Address in Commemoration of the 50th Anniversary of the Institution of the Synod of Bishops*, 17 October 2015) and provides the correct context for understanding the mandate that Christ entrusts, in the Holy Spirit, to pastors. Synodality, therefore, invites the whole Church, including those who exercise authority, to conversion and reform.

## UNITY AS HARMONY

34. "As a spiritual being, the human creature is defined through interpersonal relations. The more authentically he or she lives these relations, the more his or her own personal identity matures. It is not by isolation that man establishes his

worth, but by placing himself in relation with others and with God. Hence these relations take on fundamental importance." (CV 53). We recognise a synodal Church by flourishing interpersonal relationships flowing from the mutual love that constitutes the new commandment left by Jesus to His disciples (cf. *Jn* 13:34-35). The Church as "a people made one by the unity of the Father and the Son and the Holy Spirit" (LG 4) can witness to the power of relationships founded in the Trinity especially where individualism pervades cultures and societies. Differences that are found in every Christian community with respect to age, vocation, sex, profession and social belonging provide an opportunity for an encounter with otherness that is indispensable to personal growth and maturity.

35. Families, which the Council refers to as "as it were, the domestic Church" (LG 11), are the pre-eminent context in which we learn to live out the richness of relationships between persons, united in their diversity of character, sex, age and role. In families, we learn to experience the basic practices needed for a synodal Church. The reality of brokenness and suffering experienced by families notwithstanding, they remain places where we learn to exchange the gifts of love, trust, reconciliation, forgiveness and understanding. Here, we learn that we are equal in dignity and created for reciprocity, that we need to be listened to, and that we are able to listen. Here we first learn how to discern and decide together, accept and exercise authority that is loving and life-giving, and to be co-responsible and accountable. "Family humanises people through the relationship of 'us' and at the same time promotes the legitimate differences of each one" (Francis, *Address to the Pontifical Academy of Social Sciences*, 29 April 2022).

36. The synodal process has shown that the Holy Spirit constantly calls forth from the People of God a great variety of charisms and ministries. "In the structure of the body of Christ, too, there is a diversity of members and of functions. There is one Spirit who distributes his various gifts for the good of

the Church according to his own riches and the needs of the ministries (cf. *1 Cor* 12:1-11)" (LG 7). Equally, a desire emerged to expand possibilities for participation and for the exercise of differentiated co-responsibility by all the Baptised, men and women. In this regard, however, the lack of participation by so many members of the People of God in this journey of ecclesial renewal was a source of sadness. There was also a sense of sadness expressed at the widespread difficulty within the Church in living flourishing relationships fully between men and women, between different generations and between individuals and groups with diverse cultural identities and social conditions. Of particular concern in this regard must be those people made poor and those who are excluded.

37. In addition, the synodal process highlighted the spiritual heritage of the local Churches, in which and from which the Catholic Church exists and the need to combine their experiences. By virtue of catholicity, "the individual parts bring their own gifts to the other parts and to the whole Church, in such a way that the whole and individual parts grow greater through the mutual communication of all and their united efforts towards fullness in unity" (LG 13). The ministry of the successor of Peter "safeguards legitimate differences while taking care that what is particular not only does no harm to unity but rather is conducive to it" (*ibid.*, cf. AG 22).

38. The whole Church has always been comprised of a plurality of peoples and languages, of vocations, charisms and ministries at the service of the common good, as well as of local Churches. In turn, these local Churches have always possessed their own rites and disciplines as well as their own distinctive theological and spiritual heritage. The unity of this diversity is realised by Christ, the cornerstone, and the Holy Spirit, the source of all harmony. This unity in diversity is precisely what is meant by the catholicity of the Church. The richness of the plurality of the Churches *sui iuris* highlighted by the synodal process, is a sign of this very catholicity. The Assembly asks that we continue along

the path of the encounter, mutual understanding and exchange of gifts that nourish the communion of a Church of Churches.

39. Synodal renewal fosters an appreciation of local contexts as the place where the universal call from God manifests and fulfils itself. It is a call to be part of God's People, to participate in that Reign of God, which is "righteousness and peace and joy in the Holy Spirit" (*Rom* 14:17). In this way, different cultures are enabled to grasp the unity that underlies their plurality and become open to the prospect of an exchange of gifts. "The unity of the Church is not uniformity, but an organic blending of legitimate diversities" (NMI 46). There is a variety of ways in which the message of salvation is expressed. This helps avoid reducing this message to a single understanding of the life of the Church and of the theological, liturgical, pastoral and disciplinary forms it takes.

40. The appreciation of contexts, cultures and diversities, and of the relationships between them, is key to growing as a missionary synodal Church and to journeying, prompted by the Holy Spirit, towards the visible unity of Christians. We reaffirm the commitment of the Catholic Church to continue and intensify the ecumenical journey with other Christians by virtue of our common Baptism and in response to the call to live together the communion and unity among disciples for which Christ prayed at the Last Supper (cf. *Jn* 17:20-26). The Assembly welcomes with joy and gratitude the progress in ecumenical relations of the past sixty years, as well as the dialogue documents and declarations expressing the common faith. The participation of the Fraternal Delegates enriched the proceedings of the Assembly, and we look forward to the next steps on the path towards full communion through the incorporation of the fruits of the ecumenical journey into ecclesial practices.

41. In every place on earth, Christians live side by side with people who are not baptised yet serve God by practising a different religion. We pray solemnly for them in the liturgy of

Good Friday, and we strive together with them to build a better world, imploring the one God to free the world from the evils that afflict it. Dialogue, encounter and exchange of gifts, typical of a synodal Church, are calls to open out to relations with other religious traditions so as "to establish friendship, peace and harmony and to share spiritual and moral values and experiences in a spirit of truth and love" (Catholic Bishops' Conference of India, *Response of the Church in India to the Present-day Challenges*, 9 March 2016, cited in FT 271). In some regions, Christians who engage in building close relationships with those of other religions are subjected to persecution. The Assembly encourages them to persevere with a sense of hope.

42. The plurality of religions and cultures, the diversity of spiritual and theological traditions, the variety of the gifts of the Spirit and of the tasks of the community, as well as the diversity of age, sex and social affiliation within the Church, are an invitation to each person to recognise their particular situatedness, resist the temptation of being at the centre, and open oneself to the acceptance of other perspectives. Everyone can make a particular and indispensable contribution to completing our common task. The synodal Church can be described using the image of the orchestra: the variety of instruments is necessary to give life to the beauty and harmony of music, within which the voice of each one retains its own distinctive features at the service of the common mission. Thus, is manifested the harmony that the Spirit brings about in the Church, the One who is harmony in person (cf. St Basil, *On Psalm* 29:1; *On the Holy Spirit*, XVI: 38).

## SYNODAL SPIRITUALITY

43. Synodality is primarily a spiritual disposition. It permeates the daily life of the Baptised as well as every aspect of the Church's mission. A synodal spirituality flows from the action of the Holy Spirit and requires listening to the Word of God, contemplation, silence and conversion of heart. As Pope Francis stated in his opening address of the Second Session, "the Holy

Spirit is a sure guide and [...] our first task is to learn how to discern His voice, since He speaks through everyone and in all things" (*Address to the First General Congregation of the Second Session of the XVI General Ordinary Assembly of the Synod of Bishops*, 2 October 2024). A spirituality of synodality also requires asceticism, humility, patience and a willingness to forgive and be forgiven. It welcomes with gratitude and humility the variety of gifts and tasks distributed by the Holy Spirit for the service of the one Lord (cf. *1 Cor* 12:4-5). It does so without ambition, envy or desire for domination or control, cultivating the same attitude as Christ who "emptied himself, taking the form of a slave" (*Phil* 2:7). We recognise the fruits of a spirituality of synodality when the daily life of the Church is marked by unity and harmony in pluriformity. No one can progress along the path of authentic spirituality alone; we need support, including formation and spiritual accompaniment, both as individuals and as a community.

44. The renewal of the Christian community is possible only by recognising the primacy of grace. If spiritual depth at both personal and communal levels is lacking, synodality is reduced to organisational expediency. We are called not only to translate the fruits of a personal spiritual experience into community processes. We are also called to experience how practising the new commandment of reciprocal love is the place and form of encounter with God. In this sense, while drawing on the rich spiritual heritage of the Tradition, the synodal perspective contributes to renewing its forms: a prayer open to participation, a discernment lived together, and a missionary energy that arises from sharing and that radiates as service.

45. Conversation in the Spirit is a tool that, even with its limitations, enables listening in order to discern "what the Spirit is saying to the Churches" (*Rev* 2:7). Its practice has elicited joy, awe and gratitude and has been experienced as a path of renewal that transforms individuals, groups and the Church. The word "conversation" expresses more than mere dialogue:

it interweaves thought and feeling, creating a shared vital space. That is why we can say that conversion is at play in conversation. This is an anthropological reality found in different peoples and cultures, who gather together in solidarity to deal with and decide matters vital to the community. Grace brings this human experience to fruition. Conversing "in the Spirit" means living the experience of sharing in the light of faith and seeking God's will in an evangelical atmosphere within which the Holy Spirit's unmistakable voice can be heard.

46. The need within the Church for healing, reconciliation and the rebuilding of trust has resounded at every stage of the synodal process, particularly in light of so many scandals related to different types of abuse. It also resounded in the face of similar abuses in society. The Church is called to put at the centre of its life and action the fact that in Christ, through Baptism, we are entrusted to each other. Recognition of this profound reality becomes a sacred duty that enables us to recognise mistakes and rebuild trust. There is a missionary obligation upon the People of God to walk this path in our world and we need to invoke the gift to do so from above. Walking this path is also an act of justice. The desire to do so is the fruit of synodal renewal.

## SYNODALITY AS PROPHETIC IN TODAY'S WORLD

47. Practised with humility, the synodal style enables the Church to be a prophetic voice in today's world. "A synodal Church is like a standard lifted up among the nations (cf. *Is* 11:12)" (Francis, *Address for the Commemoration of the 50th Anniversary of the Institution of the Synod of Bishops*, 17 October 2015). We live in an age marked by ever-increasing inequalities; growing disillusionment with traditional models of governance, disenchantment with the functioning of democracy, increasing autocratic and dictatorial tendencies and the predominance of the market model without regard for the vulnerability of people and of creation. The temptation can be to resolve conflicts by force rather than by dialogue. Authentic practices of synodality

enable Christians to be a critical and prophetic voice over against the prevailing culture. In this way, we can offer a distinctive contribution to the search for answers to many challenges faced by our contemporary societies in building the common good.

48. The synodal way of living relationships is a form of testimony offered to society. It is also a way of responding to the human need to be welcomed and recognised within a particular, concrete community. The practice of synodality is a challenge to the growing isolation of people and to cultural individualism, which the Church has also often absorbed, and it calls us to mutual care, interdependence and co-responsibility for the common good. Likewise, it challenges exaggerated forms of social communitarianism that suffocate individuals and prevent them from being agents of their own development. The willingness to listen to all, especially those who are poor, stands in stark contrast to a world in which the concentration of power tends to disregard those who are poor, the marginalised, minorities and the earth, which is our common home. Synodality and integral ecology both take on the character of relationality and insist upon us nurturing what binds us together; this is why they correspond to and complement each other concerning how the mission of the Church is lived out in today's world.

# PART II - ON THE BOAT, TOGETHER

# THE CONVERSION OF RELATIONSHIPS

*Gathered there together were Simon Peter, Thomas called the Twin, Nathanael of Cana in Galilee, the sons of Zebedee, and two others of his disciples. Simon Peter said to them, 'I am going fishing.' They said to him, 'We will go with you.' (Jn 21:2-3).*

49. Lake Tiberias is where it all began. Peter, Andrew, James and John had left the boat and the nets to follow Jesus. After Easter, they set out again from that same lake. In the night, a dialogue is heard on the shore: "I am going fishing." "We will go with you." The synodal journey also began like this: we heard the invitation of Peter's successor, and we accepted it; we set out with him and followed his lead. We prayed, reflected, struggled and dialogued together. But above all we have experienced that it is relationships that sustain the Church's vitality, animating its structures. A missionary synodal Church needs to renew the one and the other.

## NEW RELATIONSHIPS

50. What emerged throughout the entire synodal journey, and in every place and context, was the call for a Church with a greater capacity to nurture relationships: with the Lord, between men and women, in the family, in the local community, among social groups and religions, with all of creation. Many participants were delighted and surprised to be asked to share their thoughts and to be given the opportunity to have their voices heard in the community. Others continued to express the pain of feeling excluded or judged because of their marital status, identity or sexuality. The desire for more real and meaningful relationships

is not only a longing to belong to a close-knit group but may also reflect a deep sense of faith. The evangelical quality of relationships in a community is decisive for the witness that the People of God are called to make in history. "By this everyone will know that you are my disciples, if you have love for one another." (*Jn* 13:35). The most eloquent sign of the Holy Spirit's action in the community of disciples is the invitation to relationship extended to those most in need, which flows from a renewal of grace and accords with the teaching of Jesus. To be a synodal Church, we are required to open ourselves to a genuine relational conversion that redirects each person's priorities, and we must once again learn from the Gospel that attending to relationships is not merely a strategy or a tool for greater organisational effectiveness. Relationships and bonds are the means by which God the Father has revealed Himself in Jesus and the Spirit. When our relationships, even in their fragility, allow the grace of Christ, the love of the Father, and the communion of the Spirit to shine through, we confess with our lives our faith in God the Trinity.

51. We should, therefore, look to the Gospels to outline for us the journey of conversion we are required to undertake, learning little by little to make Jesus's practices our own. The Gospels present to us a Lord who is often "in the act of listening to the people who come to Him along the roads of the Holy Land" (DCS 11). Jesus never sent anyone away without stopping to listen and to speak to them, whether men or women, Jews or pagans, doctors of the law or publicans, righteous men and women or sinners, beggars, the blind, lepers or the sick. By meeting people wherever their history and personal freedom had led them, He revealed to them the face of the Father. By listening to the needs and to the faith of those He met, and by responding through words and gestures, He renewed their lives, opening the path to healed relationships. Jesus is the Messiah who "even makes the deaf to hear and the mute to speak" (*Mk* 7:37). He asks us, His disciples, to do the same and, through the grace of the Holy

Spirit, gives us the capacity to do it conforming our hearts to His: only "the heart makes all authentic bonding possible, since a relationship not shaped by the heart is incapable of overcoming the fragmentation caused by individualism" (DN 17). When we listen to our sisters and brothers, we are participants in the way that God in Jesus Christ comes to meet each of us.

52. The need for conversion certainly concerns the relations between men and women. The dynamics of relationships is inscribed upon our condition as creatures. The difference between the sexes constitutes the basis of human relationships. "So God created humankind in his image [...] male and female he created them" (*Gen* 1:27). Inequality between men and women is not part of God's design. In the new creation, this difference is reconsidered in the light of the dignity of Baptism: "As many of you as were baptised into Christ have clothed yourselves with Christ. There is no longer Jew or Greek, there is no longer slave or free, there is no longer male and female; for all of you are one in Christ Jesus" (*Gal* 3:27-28). Our vocation as Christians is to welcome and respect, in every place and context, this difference, which is a gift from God and a source of life. We bear witness to the Gospel when we seek to live in relationships that respect the equal dignity and reciprocity between men and women. The widely expressed pain and suffering on the part of many women from every region and continent, both lay and consecrated, during the synodal process, reveal how often we fail to do so.

## IN A PLURALITY OF CONTEXTS

53. The call to renewed relationships in the Lord Jesus flourishes in the different contexts in which His disciples live and carry out the Church's mission. The plurality of cultures requires that the uniqueness of each cultural context is taken into account. However, all cultures are also marked by distorted relationships that are not in keeping with the Gospel. Throughout history, these relational failures have turned into structures of sin (cf. SRS 36), which in turn shape the way people think and act. In particular,

structures of sin create obstacles and generate fear. We need to face these in order to set out on the road to the conversion of relationships in the light of the Gospel.

54. The evils that plague our world, including wars and armed conflicts and the illusion that just peace can be achieved by force, are rooted in these dynamics. Just as destructive is the belief that all of creation, and this includes humans themselves, can be exploited at will for profit. A consequence of this reality is the creation of barriers that divide, including amongst Christian communities, resulting in inequalities whereby some have possibilities that are denied to others. These are inequalities such as between men and women, racial prejudices, caste divisions, discrimination against people with disabilities, violation of the rights of minorities of all kinds and the reluctance to accept migrants. Even our relationship with our mother and sister earth (cf. LS 1) bears the mark of a fracture that endangers the lives of countless communities, particularly among those most poor, if not entire peoples and perhaps all of humanity. The most radical and dramatic rejection is that of human life itself; this leads to the discarding of the unborn, as well as of the elderly.

55. Many of the evils that afflict our world are also visible in the Church. The abuse crisis, in its various and tragic manifestations, has brought untold and often ongoing suffering to victims and survivors, and to their communities. The Church needs to listen with special attention and sensitivity to the voices of victims and survivors of sexual, spiritual, economic, power and conscience abuse by members of the clergy or persons with Church appointments. Listening is a fundamental element of the path to healing, repentance, justice and reconciliation. At a time characterised by a global crisis of trust, which encourages people to live in distrust and suspicion, the Church must acknowledge its own shortcomings. It must humbly ask for forgiveness, must care for victims, provide for preventative measures, and strive in the Lord to rebuild mutual trust.

56. Listening to those who suffer exclusion and marginalisation strengthens the Church's awareness that taking on the burden of wounded relationships is part of its mission. The Church does this in order that the Lord, the Living One, can heal them. This is the only way that the Church can be "as a sacrament or instrumental sign of intimate union with God and of the unity of all humanity" (LG 1). At the same time, being open to the world allows one to discover that the Spirit has sown the seeds of the Gospel in every corner of the globe, in every culture and in every human group. These seeds bear fruit in the ability to live healthy relationships, cultivate mutual trust and forgiveness and overcome fear of diversity. They also give life to welcoming communities, promote an economy respectful of people and the planet and bring about reconciliation after conflict. History leaves us with a legacy of conflicts motivated also by religious affiliation, undermining the credibility of religions themselves. Much suffering has been caused by the scandal of division between Christian communions and the hostility between sisters and brothers who have received the same Baptism. The renewed experience of ecumenical momentum that marks the synod's journey opens the way towards hope.

## CHARISMS, VOCATIONS AND MINISTRIES FOR MISSION

57. Christians, individually and as part of ecclesial movements and associations, are called to bear fruit by sharing the gifts they have been given and to be witnesses to the Gospel. "Now there are varieties of gifts, but the same Spirit; and there are varieties of services, but the same Lord; and there are varieties of activities, but it is the same God who activates all of them in everyone. To each is given the manifestation of the Spirit for the common good" (*1 Cor* 12:4-7). In the Christian community, all the Baptised are enriched with gifts to share, each according to his or her vocation and way or condition of life. The various ecclesial vocations are many, yet they express the one Baptismal call to holiness and mission. The variety of charisms, which

originates in the freedom of the Holy Spirit, aims at unifying the ecclesial body of Christ (cf. LG 32) and promoting mission in different places and cultures (cf. LG 12). These gifts are not the exclusive property of those who receive and use them, nor are they intended solely for their personal benefit or for that of a group. Through an appropriate pastoral care for vocations, they are intended for the flourishing of the life of the Christian community and the development of society as a whole.

58. Each Baptised person responds to missionary needs in the contexts in which they live and work, according to their dispositions and abilities. This demonstrates the freedom of the Spirit in bestowing God's gifts. Owing to this dynamism in the Spirit, the People of God, listening to the reality in which they live, discover new forms of commitment and new ways to fulfil their mission. Christians, each according to their diverse roles - within the family and other states of life; in the workplace and in their professions; engaged civilly, politically, socially or ecologically; in the development of a culture inspired by the Gospel, including the evangelisation of the digital environment - walk the paths of the world and proclaim the Gospel where they live, sustained by the gifts of the Spirit.

59. In doing so, they ask the Church not to abandon them but rather to enable them to feel that they are sent and sustained in mission. They ask to be nourished by the bread of the Word and the Eucharist, as well as by the familial bonds of the community. They ask that their commitment be recognised for what it is: Church action in light of the Gospel, and not merely a personal choice. Lastly, they ask the community to accompany those who, through their witness, have been drawn to the Gospel. In a missionary synodal Church, under the leadership of their pastors, communities will be able to send people out in mission and support those they have sent. Communities will, therefore, see themselves as primarily devoted to the service of a mission that the faithful carry out within society, in family and working life. They will, therefore, not remain focused exclusively on the

activities that take place within their own communities and upon their own organisational needs.

60. By virtue of Baptism, women and men have equal dignity as members of the People of God. However, women continue to encounter obstacles in obtaining a fuller recognition of their charisms, vocation and place in all the various areas of the Church's life. This is to the detriment of serving the Church's shared mission. Scripture attests to the prominent role of many women in the history of salvation. One woman, Mary Magdalene, was entrusted with the first proclamation of the Resurrection. On the day of Pentecost, Mary, the Mother of God, was present, accompanied by many other women who had followed the Lord. It is important that the Scripture passages that relate these stories find adequate space inside liturgical lectionaries. Crucial turning points in Church history confirm the essential contribution of women moved by the Spirit. Women make up the majority of churchgoers and are often the first witnesses to the faith in families. They are active in the life of small Christian communities and parishes. They run schools, hospitals and shelters. They lead initiatives for reconciliation and promoting human dignity and social justice. Women contribute to theological research and are present in positions of responsibility in Church institutions, in diocesan curia and the Roman Curia. There are women who hold positions of authority and are leaders of their communities. This Assembly asks for full implementation of all the opportunities already provided for in Canon Law with regard to the role of women, particularly in those places where they remain under-utilised. There is no reason or impediment that should prevent women from carrying out leadership roles in the Church: what comes from the Holy Spirit cannot be stopped. Additionally, the question of women's access to diaconal ministry remains open. This discernment needs to continue. The Assembly also asks that more attention be given to the language and images used in preaching, teaching, catechesis, and the drafting of official Church documents, giving more space to the contributions of female saints, theologians and mystics.

61. Within the Christian community, special attention should be given to children. Not only do children need accompaniment in their growth, but they have much to give to the community of believers. When the apostles argue among themselves about who is the greatest, Jesus puts a child at the centre, presenting the child as a criterion for entering the Kingdom (cf. *Mk* 9:33-37). The Church cannot be synodal without the contribution of children, who are bearers of missionary potential, being valued. The voice of the child is needed by the community. We must listen to children and make efforts to ensure that everyone in society listens to them, especially those who have political and educational responsibilities. A society that is not able to welcome and care for children is a sickly society. The suffering experienced by many children due to war, poverty and abandonment, abuse and trafficking is a scandal that calls both for the courage to denounce their suffering and for a serious commitment to solidarity.

62. Young people also make a contribution to the synodal renewal of the Church. They are acutely aware of the values of fellowship and sharing while rejecting paternalism or authoritarian attitudes. At times, their attitude toward the Church can come across as critical, yet often it manifests positively as a personal commitment to the creation of a welcoming community dedicated to fighting against social injustice and for the care of our common home. The request that they made at the 2018 Synod on Young People to "walk together in daily life" corresponds exactly to the vision of a synodal Church. For this reason, it is fundamental that we assure them of thoughtful and patient accompaniment; in particular, the proposal of "an experience of accompaniment in view of discernment", which arose thanks to their contribution, deserves to be revisited and taken up again. It foresees companionship shared with educators, an apostolic commitment lived at the service of the neediest, and the offer of a spirituality rooted in prayer and the sacramental life (cf. *Final Document of the XV Ordinary General Assembly of the Synod of Bishops, "Young People, the Faith and Vocational Discernment"*, 161).

63. In promoting co-responsibility for the mission of all the Baptised, we recognise the apostolic capacities of people with disabilities who feel called and sent out as active agents of evangelisation. We appreciate the contribution that comes from the immense wealth of humanity they bring with them. We acknowledge their experiences of suffering, marginalisation, and discrimination, sometimes suffered even within the Christian community due to attempts at showing compassion that can be paternalistic. In order to encourage their participation in the life and mission of the Church, we propose the establishment of a Church-based research initiative or observatory on disability.

64. Among the vocations that enrich the Church, that of married persons stands out. The Second Vatican Council taught that "in their state and way of life, they have their own particular gift within the People of God" (LG 11). The Sacrament of Marriage assigns a distinctive mission that concerns, at the same time, the life of the family, the building up of the Church and a commitment within society. In particular, in recent years, there has been a growing awareness that when it comes to the pastoral care of families, families themselves are active participants and not just passive recipients. For this reason, families meet and network together, and Church institutions focused on the education of children and young adults may assist them in doing so. The Assembly once again expressed its closeness to and support for all those who accept being alone as a choice made in fidelity to the Church's Tradition and Magisterium on marriage and sexual ethics, which they recognise as a source of life.

65. Over the centuries, the Church has also been enriched spiritually by the many different forms of consecrated life. From the very beginning, the Church has recognised the action of the Spirit in men and women who have followed Christ along the path of the evangelical counsels, consecrating themselves to the service of God, whether through contemplation or other forms of service. They are called to interrogate Church and society with their prophetic voice. Across their centuries-long history,

the various forms of consecrated life elaborated what we now recognise as practices of synodal living. These include how to practise discernment in common and to harmonise together individual gifts as well as pursue mission in common. Orders and congregations, societies of apostolic life, secular institutes, as well as associations, movements and new communities, all have a special contribution to make to the growth of synodality in the Church. Today, many communities of consecrated life are like laboratories for inter-cultural living in a way that is prophetic for both the Church and the world. At the same time, synodality invites – and sometimes challenges – pastors of local Churches, as well as those responsible for leadership in consecrated life and in the movements, to strengthen relationships in order to bring to life an exchange of gifts at the service of the common mission.

66. Mission involves all the Baptised. The first task of lay women and men is to permeate and transform earthly realities with the spirit of the Gospel (cf. LG 31.33; AA 5-7). At the behest of Pope Francis (cf. Apostolic Letter issued "Motu Proprio" *Spiritus Domini*, 10 January 2021), the synodal process urged local Churches to respond with creativity and courage to the needs of the mission. This response should involve discernment among the various charisms in order to identify which of these should take a ministerial form and thus be equipped with adequate criteria, tools and procedures. Not all charisms need to be configured as ministries, nor do all the Baptised need to become ministers, nor do all ministries need to be instituted. For a charism to be configured as a ministry, the community must identify a genuine pastoral need. This should be accompanied by a discernment carried out by the pastor, who, together with the community, will make a decision on whether there is a need to create a new ministry. As a result of this process, the competent authority reaches a decision. A missionary synodal Church would encourage more forms of lay ministries, that is, ministries that do not require the sacrament of Holy Orders, and this not only within the liturgical sphere. They can be instituted

or not instituted. Further reflection should be given to the most effective way of bestowing lay ministries at a time when people move from one place to another with increasing ease, specifying the times and areas of their exercise.

67. Among the many ecclesial services recognised by the Assembly was the contribution to the understanding of the faith and discernment offered by theology in the variety of its expressions. Theologians help the People of God to develop an understanding of reality enlightened by Revelation and to develop suitable responses and the appropriate language for mission. In the synodal and missionary Church, "the charism of theology is called to offer a specific service [...]. Together with the faithful People's experience of faith and contemplation of the truth, and with the preaching of the Pastors, theology contributes to an ever deeper penetration into the Gospel. Furthermore, 'As in the case of all Christian vocations, the ministry of theologians, as well as being personal, is also both communal and collegial'" (ITC 75). This ministry is particularly communitarian and collegial when carried out as teaching entrusted with a canonical mission in ecclesiastical academic institutions. "Ecclesial synodality therefore needs theologians to do theology in a synodal way, developing their capacity to listen to each other, to dialogue, to discern and to harmonise their many and varied approaches and contributions" (*ibid.*). In this view, it is urgent to foster dialogue between Pastors and those engaged in theological research according to appropriate institutional forms. The Assembly invites theological institutions to continue research aimed at clarifying and deepening the meaning of synodality and accompanying formation in the local Churches.

## ORDAINED MINISTERS AT THE SERVICE OF HARMONY

68. As with all ministries in the Church, the episcopate, priesthood and diaconate are at the service of proclaiming the Gospel and building up the ecclesial community. The Second

Vatican Council recalled that the divinely established ordained ministry "is exercised in different orders by those who right from ancient times are called Bishops, Priests and Deacons" (LG 28). In this context, the Second Vatican Council affirmed the sacramentality of the episcopate (cf. LG 21), recovered the communion of the presbyterate (cf. LG 28) and paved the way for the restoration of the permanent exercise of the diaconate in the Latin Church (cf. LG 29).

*The Bishop's ministry: integrating the gifts of the Spirit in unity*

69. A Bishop's task is to preside over a local Church as a visible principle of unity within it and a bond of communion with all the Churches. The Council's affirmation that "the fullness of the sacrament of order is conferred by episcopal consecration" (LG 21) allows us to understand the identity of the Bishop in the framework of sacramental relations with Christ and with the "portion of the People of God" (CD 11). The Bishop is called to serve this portion of the people entrusted to him in the name of Christ the Good Shepherd. He who is ordained Bishop is not charged with prerogatives and tasks that he must perform alone. Rather, he receives the grace and the task of recognising, discerning and bringing together in unity the gifts that the Spirit pours out on individuals and communities, working with Priests and Deacons in a way that reflects their common sacramental bond; they are co-responsible with him for ministerial service in the local Church. In doing this, the Bishop realises what is most proper and specific to his mission in the context of his solicitude for the communion of Churches.

70. A Bishop's service is a service in, with and for the community (cf. LG 20). It is carried out through the proclamation of the Word and by presiding over the celebration of the Eucharist and the other sacraments. This is why the Synodal Assembly desires that the People of God have a greater voice in choosing Bishops. It also recommends that the ordination of a Bishop should take place in the diocese to which he is destined as pastor, and not in his home diocese, as is often the case. It also recommends

that the principal consecrator be chosen from among the Bishops of the ecclesiastical province, including, as far as possible, the Metropolitan. It will thus become clearer that he who becomes a Bishop establishes a bond with the Church to which he is destined, publicly assuming before it the commitments of his ministry. It is equally important that, especially during pastoral visits, the Bishop can spend time with the faithful to listen to them as part of his own ongoing discernment of needs. This will also assist them in experiencing the Church as God's family. In the case of titular Bishops today, the constitutive relationship between the Bishop and the local Church does not appear with sufficient clarity, for example, in the case of papal representatives, those who serve in the Roman Curia and auxiliary Bishops. It would be opportune to continue to reflect upon this matter.

71. Bishops also need to be accompanied and supported in their ministry. The Metropolitan Bishop can play a role in promoting fraternity among Bishops of neighbouring dioceses. During the course of the synod, the need emerged to offer Bishops ongoing formation paths, including in local contexts. The need also surfaced to clarify the role of auxiliary Bishops and to expand the tasks that Bishops can delegate. The experience of Bishops *emeriti* in their new way of being at the service of the People of God should also be taken into consideration. It is important to help the faithful to avoid excessive and unrealistic expectations of the Bishop, remembering that he too is a fragile brother, exposed to temptation, in need of help like everyone else. An idealised image of the ministry of the Bishop, which is a delicate and sensitive one, makes performing it more difficult. On the other hand, his ministry is greatly enhanced when, in a truly synodal Church, it is supported by the active participation of all the People of God.

*With the Bishop: Priests and Deacons*

72. In a synodal Church, Priests are called to live their service in a spirit of proximity to their people, to be welcoming and prepared to listen to all, opening themselves up to a synodal style.

Priests "constitute along with their Bishop one presbyterium" (LG 28) and collaborate with him in discerning charisms and in accompanying and guiding the local Church with particular regard to the matter of safeguarding unity. They are called to live in solidarity with their brother Priests and to collaborate in providing pastorally for their people. Priests who belong to religious orders and congregations enrich the presbyterium with the uniqueness of their charism. These, along with Priests who come from Eastern Churches *sui iuris*, be they celibate or married, the *fidei donum* Priests, and those who come from other countries, assist the local clergy in opening themselves to a whole Church perspective. In turn, local Priests help clergy from elsewhere to become part of the history of a concrete diocese with its distinctive spiritual richness and traditions. In this way, the presbyterium, too, experiences a genuine exchange of gifts in the service of the Church's mission. Priests also need to be accompanied and supported, especially in the early stages of their ministry as well as at times of weakness and fragility.

73. Servants of the mystery of God and the Church (cf. LG 41), Deacons are ordained "not for the priesthood but for the ministry" (LG 29). They exercise this ministry in the service of charity, in proclamation and in the liturgy. In doing so they make real the relation between the Gospel and a life lived in love in every social and Church context. They also promote within the whole Church both a consciousness of service and a particular style of service towards all, especially the poorest. As the Tradition, the prayer of ordination and pastoral practice demonstrate, the functions of Deacons are many. Deacons respond to the specific needs of each local Church, particularly reawakening and sustaining everyone's attention to the poorest in a Church which is synodal, missionary and merciful. The ministry of Deacons remains unknown to many Christians, in part because, although it was restored by Vatican II in the Latin Church as a distinct and permanent grade (cf. LG 29), it has not been welcomed in every part of the world. The teaching of the

Council needs to be more deeply explored, particularly in the light of a review of the lived experience of the diaconate. This teaching already offers good reasons to local Churches not to delay in promoting the permanent diaconate more generously, recognising in this ministry a valuable resource in the growth of a servant Church, following the example of the Lord Jesus, who made Himself the servant of all. This deeper understanding could also help to better comprehend the meaning of the diaconal ordination of those who will become Priests.

*Collaboration between ordained ministers within a Synodal Church*

74. Frequently, during the synodal process, the Bishops, Priests and Deacons were thanked for the joy, commitment and dedication with which they carry out their service. Often mentioned, in addition, were the very real difficulties encountered by pastors in their ministry. These mainly concerned a sense of isolation and loneliness, as well as the feeling of being overwhelmed by the expectation that they are required to fulfil every need. The experience of the Synod can be a response to this reality, helping Bishops, Priests and Deacons to rediscover co-responsibility in the exercise of ministry, which includes collaboration with other members of the People of God. A wider distribution of tasks and responsibilities and a more courageous discernment of what properly belongs to the ordained ministry and what can and must be delegated to others will enable each ministry to be exercised in a more spiritually sound and pastorally dynamic manner. This perspective will surely have an impact on decision-making processes, enabling them to have a more clearly synodal character. It will also help to overcome clericalism, understood as the use of power to one's own advantage and the distortion of the authority of the Church that is at the service of the People of God. This expresses itself above all in forms of abuse, be they sexual or economic, the abuse of conscience and of power, by ministers of the Church. "Clericalism, whether fostered by Priests themselves or by lay persons, leads to an excision in the

ecclesial body that supports and helps to perpetuate many of the evils that we are condemning today" (Francis, *Letter to the People of God*, 20 August 2018).

## TOGETHER FOR MISSION

75. Throughout its history, the Church has adopted other ministries apart from those of the ordained in response to the needs of the community and the mission. Charisms take the form of ministries when they are publicly recognised by the community and by those responsible for leading the community. In this way, they are placed at the service of the mission in a stable and consistent way. Some tend, more specifically, towards service of the Christian community. Of particular importance are instituted ministries. These are conferred by a Bishop once in a lifetime through a specific rite and after appropriate discernment and formation of the candidates. These ministries cannot be reduced to a simple mandate or assignment of tasks. The conferral of ministry is a sacramental that shapes the person and redefines his or her way of participating in the life and mission of the Church. In the Latin Church, these are the ministries of lector and acolyte (cf. Francis, Apostolic Letter issued "Motu Proprio" *Spiritus Domini*, 10 January 2021) and that of the catechist (cf. Francis, Apostolic Letter issued "Motu Proprio" *Antiquum Ministerium*, 10 May 2021). A legitimate authority establishes the terms and conditions of their practice by mandate. Episcopal Conferences establish the personal conditions that candidates for these ministries must fulfil and draw up the formation pathways that must be taken to access these ministries.

76. Instituted ministries are complemented by those not instituted by ritual but are exercised with stability as mandated by the competent authority. Some examples of such ministries include the ministry of co-ordinating a small Church community, leading community prayer, organising charitable activities, and so forth. These ministries have a great variety of expressions depending on the characteristics of the local community. An

example is the catechists who, in many regions of Africa, have always been responsible for communities without Priests. Although there is no prescribed rite, in order to promote its effective recognition, a public entrustment should be made through a mandate before the community. There are also extraordinary ministries, including the extraordinary ministry of the Eucharist, leading Sunday liturgies in the absence of a Priest, administering certain sacramentals, and other instances. The canons of the Latin and Eastern Churches already provide that, in certain cases, the lay faithful, men or women, may also be extraordinary ministers of Baptism. In the Latin canons, the Bishop (with the Holy See's authorisation) may delegate assistance at marriages to lay faithful, men or women. Responsive to the needs of local contexts, consideration should be given to extending and stabilising these opportunities for the exercise of lay ministries. Finally, there are spontaneous services, which need no further conditions or explicit recognition. They demonstrate that all the faithful, in various ways, participate in the mission through their gifts and charisms.

77. The lay faithful, both men and women, should be given greater opportunities for participation, also exploring new forms of service and ministry in response to the pastoral needs of our time in a spirit of collaboration and differentiated co-responsibility. In particular, some concrete needs have emerged from the synodal process. These ought to be responded to according to the various contexts:

a) increased participation of laymen and laywomen in Church discernment processes and all phases of decision-making processes (drafting, making and confirming decisions);

b) greater access of laymen and laywomen to positions of responsibility in dioceses and ecclesiastical institutions, including seminaries, theological institutes and faculties, more fully enacting existing provisions;

c) greater recognition and support for the lives and charisms of consecrated men and women and their employment in positions of ecclesial responsibility;

d) a greater number of qualified lay people serving as judges in all canonical processes;

e) effective recognition of the dignity and respect for the rights of those who are employed in the Church and its institutions.

78. The synodal process has renewed the awareness that listening is an essential component of every aspect of the Church's life: administering sacraments, in particular that of Reconciliation, catechesis, formation and pastoral accompaniment. In this light, the Assembly also focused on the proposal to establish a ministry of listening and accompaniment, showing a variety of perspectives. Some were in favour of this proposal because this ministry would represent a prophetic way of emphasising the importance of listening and accompaniment in the community. Others said that listening and accompaniment are the tasks of all the Baptised, without there being the need for a specific ministry. Others still underlined the need for further study, for example, of the relationship between this ministry of listening and accompaniment and spiritual accompaniment, pastoral counselling, and the celebration of the Sacrament of Reconciliation. It was also proposed that a possible 'ministry of listening and accompaniment' should be particularly aimed at welcoming those who are on the margins of the Church community, those who return after having drifted away and those who are searching for the truth and wish to be helped to meet the Lord. Therefore, in this regard, discernment should continue. The local contexts where this need is more strongly felt can try to explore possible approaches upon which to base a discernment.

# PART III – "CAST THE NET"
# THE CONVERSION OF PROCESSES

*Jesus said to them, "Children, you have no fish, have you?" They answered him, "No." He said to them, "Cast the net to the right side of the boat, and you will find some." So they cast it, and now they were not able to haul it in because there were so many fish. (Jn 21:5-6).*

79. The fishing has not borne fruit, and it is now time to return to shore. Yet a voice rings out, in an authoritative tone, inviting the disciples to do something that they alone would not have done, pointing to a possibility that their eyes and minds could not grasp: "Cast the net to the right side of the boat, and you will find some." During this synodal journey, we have sought to hear this Voice and to welcome it. In prayer and dialogue, we have recognised that ecclesial discernment, the care for decision-making processes, the commitment to accountability and the evaluation of our decisions are practices through which we respond to the Word that shows us the paths of mission.

80. These three practices are closely intertwined. Decision-making processes need ecclesial discernment, which requires listening in a climate of trust that is supported by transparency and accountability. Trust must be mutual: decision-makers need to be able to trust and listen to the People of God. The latter, in turn, needs to be able to trust those in authority. This integral vision highlights that each of these practices depends on and supports the others, thus serving the Church's ability to fulfil its mission. Formation is needed in order to engage in decision-making processes grounded in ecclesial discernment and which reflect a culture of transparency, accountability and evaluation. The formation required is not only technical; it also needs to

explore theological, biblical and spiritual foundations. All the Baptised need this formation in witness, mission, holiness and service, which emphasises co-responsibility. It takes on particular forms for those in positions of responsibility or at the service of ecclesial discernment.

## ECCLESIAL DISCERNMENT FOR MISSION

81. In order to promote relationships capable of sustaining and orienting the mission of the Church, a priority must be made to exercise the evangelical wisdom that allowed the apostolic community of Jerusalem to seal the result of the first synodal event using the following words: "For it has seemed good to the Holy Spirit and to us" (*Acts* 15:28). This is discernment that can be qualified as "ecclesial," since it is the People of God that undertake it in view of mission. The Spirit, whom the Father sends in Jesus's name and who teaches everything (cf. *Jn* 14:26), guides believers in every age "into all the truth" (*Jn* 16:13). Through the Spirit's presence and enduring action, the "tradition which comes from the apostles progresses in the Church" (DV 8). Calling on the Spirit's light, the People of God, who participate in the prophetic function of Christ (cf. LG 12), "works to discern the true signs of God's presence and purpose in the events, needs and desires which it shares with the rest of modern humanity" (GS 11). This discernment draws on all the gifts of wisdom that the Lord bestows upon the Church and on the *sensus fidei* bestowed upon all the Baptised by the Spirit. In this Spirit, the life of a missionary and synodal Church must be re-envisioned and re-orientated.

82. Ecclesial discernment is not an organisational technique but rather a spiritual practice grounded in a living faith. It calls for interior freedom, humility, prayer, mutual trust, an openness to the new and a surrender to the will of God. It is never just a setting out of one's own personal or group point of view or a summing up of differing individual opinions. Each person, speaking according to their conscience, is called to open

themselves to the others who share according to their conscience. In this sharing, they seek to recognise together "what the Spirit is saying to the Churches" (*Rev* 2:7). As ecclesial discernment entails the contribution of everyone, it is both the condition and a privileged expression of synodality, in which communion, mission and participation are lived. The more everyone is heard, the richer the discernment. Therefore, it is essential that we promote the broadest participation possible in the discernment process, particularly involving those who are at the margins of the Christian community and society.

83. Listening to the Word of God is the starting point and criterion for all ecclesial discernment. The Scriptures testify that God has spoken to His People to the point of giving us in Jesus the fullness of all Revelation (cf. DV 2). They indicate the places where we can hear His voice. God communicates with us first of all in the liturgy because it is Christ himself who speaks "when scripture is read in the Church" (SC 7). God speaks through the living Tradition of the Church, the Magisterium, personal and communal meditation on the Scriptures, and the practices of popular piety. God continues to manifest Himself through the cry of those who are made poor and in the events of human history. God also communicates with His People through the elements of Creation, whose very existence points to the Creator's action and which is filled with the presence of the life-giving Spirit. Finally, God also speaks through the personal conscience of each person, which is "the most intimate centre and sanctuary of a person, in which he or she is alone with God and whose voice echoes within them." (GS 16). Ecclesial discernment demands the continuous care for and formation of consciences and the maturing of the *sensus fidei*, so as not to neglect any of the places where God speaks and comes to meet His People.

84. The steps of ecclesial discernment will differ depending on the various places and their traditions. Based on the synodal experience, we have identified some elements of discernment which should be included:

a) clearly setting out the object of discernment and disseminating information and the means for adequately understanding it;

b) giving sufficient time for prayerful preparation, for listening to the Word of God and for reflection on the question;

c) an inner disposition of freedom regarding one's own interests, both personal and as a group, and a commitment to the pursuit of the common good;

d) listening attentively and respectfully to each person's voice;

e) searching for the widest possible consensus which will emerge when our hearts burn within us (cf. *Lk* 24:32), without hiding conflicts or searching for the lowest common denominator;

f) the leaders of the process formulate the consensus in such a way that allows the participants to say whether they recognise themselves in it or not.

The discernment process should lead to a mature acceptance by all of the decision, even by those whose individual opinions are not accepted. The process should also provide for a period for reception by the community that will lead to further review and assessment.

85. Discernment always unfolds within a particular context, the complexities and specificities of which must be grasped as completely as possible. For discernment to be truly 'ecclesial', it should make use of the appropriate means. These include an adequate biblical exegesis to help interpret and understand biblical texts while avoiding partial or fundamentalist interpretations; a knowledge of the Fathers of the Church, of Tradition and the teachings of the Magisterium, according to their varying degrees of authority; the contributions of the various theological disciplines; and the contributions of the human, historical, social and administrative sciences. Without these latter, it is not possible to grasp the context in which and with a view to which discernment takes place.

86. The Church enjoys a wide variety of approaches to and well-established methods of discernment. This variety is a gift as it allows adaptation to different contexts and shows itself to be fruitful. Keeping our common mission in view, we should bring these different approaches into dialogue, ensuring that neither loses its specific character nor becomes fixed in its way of proceeding. It is essential to offer formation opportunities that spread and nourish a culture of ecclesial discernment focused on mission in local Churches, starting from small ecclesial communities and parishes. This is particularly necessary amongst those who hold leadership roles. It is equally important to encourage the formation of facilitators, whose contribution is often crucial to the process of discernment.

## THE STRUCTURE OF THE DECISION-MAKING PROCESS

87. In the synodal Church "the whole community, in the free and rich diversity of its members, is called together to pray, listen, analyse, dialogue, discern and offer advice on taking pastoral decisions" (ITC 68) for mission. The way to promote a synodal Church is to foster as great a participation of all the People of God as possible in decision-making processes. If it is indeed true that the Church's very way of living and operating is synodal, then this practice is essential to the Church's mission, requiring discernment, the reaching of consensus, and decision-making through the use of the various structures and institutions of synodality.

88. The community of disciples convoked and sent by the Lord is neither uniform nor shapeless. It is His Body composed of diverse members, a community with a history within which the Reign of God is present as a "seed and beginning" at the service of His coming amongst the whole human family (cf. LG 5). The Fathers of the Church reflect on the communal nature of the mission of the People of God with a triple "nothing without": "nothing without the Bishop" (St Ignatius of Antioch, *Letter to*

*the Trallians* 2,2) "nothing without your advice [of Presbyters and Deacons] and the consent of the People" (St Cyprian of Carthage, *Letter to the Brothers Presbyters and Deacons*, 14,4). When this logic of "nothing without" is disregarded, the identity of the Church is obscured, and its mission is hindered.

89. This ecclesiological framework shapes the commitment to promote participation based on differentiated co-responsibility. Each member of the community must be respected, with value placed upon their gifts and abilities in light of the goal of shared decision-making. More or less sophisticated institutional arrangements are required to facilitate this process depending on the size of the community. The current law already provides for such participatory bodies at various levels. These will be dealt with later in the document.

90. It is appropriate to reflect on decision-making processes to ensure their effective functionality. These processes typically involve a period of elaboration and preparation "through a joint exercise of discernment, consultation and co-operation" (ITC 69), which informs and underpins the subsequent taking of a decision by the competent authority. There is no competition or conflict between the two elements of the process; rather, they both contribute to ensuring that the decisions taken are the fruit of the obedience of all to what God wants for His Church. For this reason, it is necessary to encourage procedures that make reciprocity between the assembly and the person presiding effective in an atmosphere of openness to the Spirit and mutual trust in search of a consensus that could, possibly, be unanimous. Once the decision has been reached, it requires a process of implementation and evaluation in which the various participants are once again involved, yet in new ways.

91. Those in authority are, in several instances, obligated by current law to conduct a consultation before taking a decision. Those with pastoral authority are obliged to listen to those who participate in the consultation and may not act as if the

consultation had not taken place. Therefore, those in authority will not depart from the fruits of consultation that produce an agreement without a compelling reason (cf. CIC, can. 127, § 2, 2°; CCEO can. 934, § 2, 3°) which must be appropriately explained. As in any community that lives according to justice, the exercise of authority in the Church does not consist in an arbitrary imposition of will. Rather, authority should always be exercised in service of communion and the reception of Christ, who is the truth towards whom the Holy Spirit guides us in different moments and contexts (cf. *Jn* 14:16).

92. In a synodal Church, the authority of the Bishop, of the Episcopal College and of the Bishop of Rome in regard to decision-taking is inviolable as it is grounded in the hierarchical structure of the Church established by Christ; it both serves unity and legitimate diversity (cf. LG 13). Such an exercise of authority, however, is not without limits: it may not ignore a direction which emerges through proper discernment within a consultative process, especially if this is done by participatory bodies. It is not appropriate to set the consultative and deliberative elements involved in reaching a decision in opposition to each other: in the Church, the deliberative element is undertaken with the help of all and never without those whose pastoral governance allows them to take a decision by virtue of their office. For this reason, the recurring formula in the Code of Canon Law, "merely consultative" vote (*tantum consultivum*) should be reviewed to eliminate the possibility of ambiguity. It seems appropriate to carry out a revision of Canon Law from a synodal perspective, clarifying the distinction and relation between consultation and deliberation and shedding light on the responsibilities of those who play different roles in the decision-making process.

93. It is of fundamental importance, if the processes of decision-making envisaged here are to bear fruit, that they be conducted in an orderly manner and that the people involved assume their own responsibilities:

a) in particular, it is up to the relevant authority to: clearly define the object of the consultation and deliberation, as well as clarify with whom ultimate responsibility for taking the decision resides. They need to identify those who ought to be consulted, including those who have a specific competency or are affected by the matter under consideration. They also need to ensure that everyone involved has access to relevant data so that they may make an informed contribution to the process;

b) those who are consulted, whether individually or as members of a collegial body, assume the responsibility of: offering their input honestly, sincerely, with an informed conscience and acting in good conscience, respecting the confidentiality of the information received, offering clearly formulated thoughts that identify their main points. This will enable the pastoral authority to explain how they have taken the consultation into account should the decision differ from the opinions offered;

c) finally, when the competent authority has formulated the decision, having respected the consultation process and clearly expressed the reasons for it, by reason of the bond of communion that unites them, all the Baptised should respect and implement the decision. They should do this even if it differs from their own opinion, but they should also be free to participate honestly in the evaluative phase. There is always a possibility of making an appeal to the higher authority according to the provision of the law.

94. Implementing the processes of decision-making correctly and resolutely, and in a synodal style, will further the progress of the People of God in a participatory way, especially by utilising the institutional means provided for in Canon Law, in particular participatory bodies. Without concrete changes in the short term, the vision of a synodal Church will not be credible, and this will alienate those members of the People of God who have drawn

strength and hope from the synodal journey. Local Churches need to find ways to implement these changes.

## TRANSPARENCY, ACCOUNTABILITY AND EVALUATION

95. Decision-making does not conclude the discernment process. It must be accompanied and followed by practices of accountability and evaluation undertaken in a spirit of transparency inspired by evangelical criteria. Accountability to the community for one's ministry belongs to our oldest tradition: to the Apostolic Church itself. Chapter Eleven of the *Acts of the Apostles* offers us the example of Peter's being held to account upon his return to Jerusalem for baptising Cornelius, a Gentile, when "the circumcised believers criticised him, saying, 'Why did you go to uncircumcised men and eat with them?'" (*Acts* 11:2-3). Peter responded by setting out the reasons for his decision.

96. In particular, it has been requested that greater light be shed on the meaning of transparency. The synodal process has connected it to words such as truth, loyalty, clarity, honesty, integrity, consistency, rejection of obscurity, hypocrisy and ambiguity, and absence of ulterior motives. The Gospel blessing of those who are "pure in heart" (*Mt* 5:8) and the command to be "innocent as doves" (*Mt* 10:16) resonated in this regard as well the words of the Apostle Paul: "We have renounced the shameful things that one hides; we refuse to practise cunning or to falsify God's word; but by the open statement of the truth we commend ourselves to the conscience of everyone in the sight of God" (*2 Cor* 4:2). Thus, when we speak of transparency we are referring to a fundamental attitude grounded in the Sacred Scriptures and not to a series of administrative or procedural requirements. Transparency, in its correct evangelical sense, does not compromise respect for privacy and confidentiality, the protection of persons, their dignity and rights, even in the face of unreasonable demands of civil authorities. However, this privacy can never legitimate practices contrary to the Gospel or become

a pretext for a cover-up or to circumvent actions to combat evil. With regard to the seal of the confessional, "The sacramental seal is indispensable and no human power has jurisdiction over it, nor can lay any claim to it." (Francis, *Address to Participants at the course organised by the Apostolic Penitentiary*, 29 March 2019)

97. The attitude to transparency we have just outlined safeguards the trust and credibility needed by a synodal Church that is attentive to relationships. When this trust is violated, the weakest and the most vulnerable suffer the most. Wherever the Church enjoys trust, the practice of transparency, accountability and evaluation helps to strengthen its credibility. These practices are even more critical where the Church's credibility needs rebuilding. They are particularly important in regard to the safeguarding of minors and vulnerable adults.

98. These practices contribute to keeping the Church faithful to its mission. The absence of these practices is one of the consequences of clericalism, which is thus fuelled. Clericalism is based on the implicit assumption that those who have authority in the Church are not to be held to account for their actions and decisions as if they were isolated from or above the rest of the People of God. Transparency and accountability should not only be invoked when it comes to sexual, financial and other forms of abuse. These practices also concern the lifestyle of pastors, pastoral planning, methods of evangelisation, and the way in which the Church respects human dignity, for example, in regard to the working conditions within its institutions.

99. If the synodal Church wants to be welcoming, then the culture and praxis of accountability must shape its actions at all levels. However, those in positions of authority have greater responsibility in this regard and are called to account for it to God and to His People. While accountability to one's superiors has been practised over the centuries, the dimension of authority's being accountable to the community is in need of restoration. The structures and procedures established through

the experience of consecrated life (such as chapters, canonical visitations, etc.) can serve as an inspiration in this regard.

100. Similarly, it is necessary to have structures and methods for regularly evaluating the exercise of ministry. Such evaluation is not a judgement upon an individual. Rather, it allows a way of assisting the minister by highlighting positive aspects of their ministry and bringing to light areas for improvement. The evaluation also assists the local Church in learning from experience, adjusting plans of action, determining the outcomes of its decisions in relation to its mission, and remaining attentive to the voice of the Holy Spirit.

101. Local Churches and their groupings are responsible for developing effective forms and processes of accountability and evaluation in a synodal way in addition to adhering to the criteria and oversight of structures already established by canonical norms. These should be appropriate to the context, including the requirements of civil law, the legitimate expectations of society and the availability of experts in the field. It is also necessary to draw on the skills of those, especially laypeople, who have greater expertise regarding accountability and evaluation. Best practices within civil society should be discerned and adapted for use within Church contexts. The way in which accountability and evaluation processes are implemented at the local level should be included in the report presented during the visits *ad limina*.

102. It seems necessary to ensure, at the very least, the establishment everywhere of the following in forms appropriate to different contexts:

a) effective functioning of finance councils;

b) effective involvement of the People of God, in particular of the more competent members, in pastoral and financial planning;

c) preparation and publication (appropriate to the local context and in an accessible form) of an annual financial report, insofar as possible externally audited, demonstrating the transparency of how the temporal goods and financial resources of the Church and its institutions are being managed;

d) the preparation and publication of an annual report on the carrying out of the local Church's mission, including also safeguarding initiatives (the protection of minors and vulnerable adults), and progress made in promoting the laity's access to positions of authority and to decision-making processes, specifying the proportion of men and women;

e) periodic evaluations of all the ministries and roles within the Church.

We need to realise that this is not a bureaucratic task for its own sake. It is rather a communication effort that proves to be a powerful educational tool for bringing about a change in culture. It also enables us to give greater visibility to many valuable initiatives of the Church and its institutions, which too often remain hidden.

## SYNODALITY AND PARTICIPATORY BODIES

103. The Baptised participate in decision-making, accountability and evaluation processes through institutional structures, primarily through those already provided for the local Church set out in the existing Code of Canon Law. In the Latin Church these are: Diocesan Synod (cf. CIC, can. 466), Presbyteral Council (cf. CIC, can. 500, § 2), Diocesan Pastoral Council (cf. CIC, can. 514, § 1), Parish Pastoral Council (cf. CIC, can. 536), Diocesan and Parish Finance Council (cf. CIC, cann. 493 e 537). In the Eastern Catholic Churches these are: Eparchial Assembly (cf. CCEO, cann. 235 ss.), Eparchial Finance Council (cf. CCEO, cann. 262 ss.), Presbyteral Council (cf. CCEO can. 264), Eparchial Pastoral Council (cf. CCEO cann. 272 ss.), Parish Councils (cf. CCEO can. 295). Members participate on the basis

of their ecclesial role and their differentiated responsibilities and capacities (charisms, ministries, experiences, competencies, etc). Each of these bodies plays a role in the discernment needed for the inculturated proclamation of the Gospel, for the community's mission in its milieu, and for the witness of the Baptised. They also contribute to the decision-making processes through established means. These bodies themselves become the subject of accountability and evaluation, as they will need to give an account of their work. Participatory bodies represent one of the most promising areas in which to act for rapid implementation of the synodal guidelines, bringing about perceptible changes speedily.

104. A synodal Church is based upon the existence, efficiency and effective vitality of these participatory bodies, not on the merely nominal existence of them. This requires that they function in accordance with canonical provisions or legitimate customs and with respect to the statutes and regulations that govern them. For this reason, we insist that they be made mandatory, as was requested at all stages of the synodal process, and that they can fully play their role, and not just in a purely formal way in a manner appropriate to their diverse local contexts.

105. Furthermore, the structure and operations of these bodies need to be addressed. It is necessary to start by adopting a synodal working method. Conversation in the Spirit, after appropriate adaptation, may constitute a reference point. Particular attention should be given to the way members are selected. When no election is envisaged, a synodal consultation should be carried out that expresses as much as possible the reality of the community or the local Church, and the relevant authority should proceed to the appointment on the basis of its results, respecting the relation between consultation and deliberation described above. It is also necessary to ensure that members of diocesan and parish pastoral councils are able to propose agenda items in an analogous way to that allowed for in the presbyteral council.

106. Equal attention needs to be given to the membership of the participatory bodies so as to encourage greater involvement by women, young people, and those living in poverty or on the margins. Furthermore, it is essential that these bodies include Baptised who are committed to living their faith in the ordinary realities of life, who are recognisably committed to an apostolic and missionary life, not only those engaged with organising ecclesial life and services internally. In this way, the ecclesial discernment will benefit from a greater openness, an ability to analyse reality and a plurality of perspectives. It may be appropriate to provide for the participation of delegates from other Churches and Christian Communions, as happened during this Synodal Assembly, or representatives of the religions present in a territory. Local Churches and their groupings can more appropriately indicate criteria for the composition of participatory bodies suitable to each context.

107. The Assembly paid special attention to best practices and positive experiences of reform. These include creating networks of pastoral councils within communities, parishes, pastoral areas, and among diocesan pastoral councils. The regular hosting of ecclesial assemblies at all levels is also encouraged. Without limiting consultation to members of the Catholic Church, these gatherings should be open to listening to the contributions from other Churches and Christian Communions. Attention should also be paid to other religions in the territory.

108. The Assembly proposes that the diocesan Synod and eparchial Assembly be more highly valued as bodies for regular consultation between the Bishop and the portion of the People of God entrusted to him. This should be the place for listening, prayer and discernment, particularly when it comes to choices pertaining to the life and mission of a local Church. Moreover, the diocesan Synod may provide scope for the exercise of accountability and evaluation whereby the Bishop gives an account of pastoral activity in various areas: the implementation of a diocesan pastoral plan, reception of the synodal processes

of the entire Church, initiatives in safeguarding and the administration of finances and temporal goods. It is, therefore, necessary to strengthen the existing canonical provisions in order to better reflect the missionary synodal character of each local Church, making provision that these bodies meet on a regular, and not rare or infrequent, basis.

# PART IV - AN ABUNDANT CATCH

# THE CONVERSION OF BONDS

*The other disciples came in the boat, dragging the net full of fish* [...]. *Simon Peter went aboard and hauled the net ashore, full of large fish, a hundred and fifty-three of them; and though there were so many, the net was not torn.* (*Jn 21:8.11*).

109. The nets cast upon the Word of the Risen One yielded a bountiful catch. All the disciples work together, hauling in the net; Peter plays a particular role. In the Gospel, fishing is an action undertaken together: everybody has their own particular task, different but co-ordinated with the others. This is the synodal Church in action – it is founded on bonds of communion that unite us and with space for all peoples and all cultures. In a time when there is great change occurring in the way we conceive of the places where the Church is rooted and on pilgrimage, we need to cultivate new forms of the exchange of gifts and the network of bonds that unite us. In this, we are sustained by the ministry of the Bishops in communion amongst themselves and with the Bishop of Rome.

## FIRMLY ROOTED YET PILGRIMS

110. The proclamation of the Gospel awakens faith in the hearts of men and women and leads to the foundation of the Church in a particular place. The Church cannot be understood apart from its roots in a specific territory, in that space and time where a shared experience of encounter with the saving God occurs. This local dimension to our Church preserves the rich diversity of expressions of faith that are grounded in a specific cultural and historical milieu. The communion of local Churches is the expression of the unity of the faithful within the one Church. Thus,

synodal conversion calls each person to enlarge the space of their heart, the heart being the first place where all our relationships resonate, grounded in each believer's personal relationship with Jesus Christ and His Church. This is the starting point and the condition of any synodal reform of the bonds of our communion and the spaces where we are Church. Pastoral action cannot be limited to tending to relationships between people who already feel attuned to one another but rather encourage the encounter between all men and women.

111. The experience of rootedness means grappling with profound socio-cultural changes that are transforming the understanding of place. 'Place' can no longer be conceived in purely geographical and spatial terms but evokes, in our time, one's belonging to a network of relationships and to a culture whose territorial roots are more dynamic and flexible than ever before. Urbanisation is one of the main factors driving this change. Today, for the first time in human history, most of the global population lives in cities. Large cities are often urban masses without a history and identity in which people live an isolated existence. Traditional territorial bonds are being redefined, blurring the borders of dioceses and parishes. Living in such contexts, the Church is called to rebuild community life, to put a face to faceless entities and to strengthen relationships in this milieu. To this end, we must not only continue to value still useful structures; we also need "missionary creativity" to explore new forms of pastoral action and identify concrete processes of care. It remains the case that rural contexts, some of which constitute genuine existential peripheries, must not be neglected and require specific pastoral attention, as do places of marginalisation and exclusion.

112. For a variety of reasons, our times are marked by a growth in population mobility. Refugees and migrants often form dynamic communities, including of religious practice, rendering multicultural the places in which they settle. Some maintain strong bonds with their country of origin, especially

with the help of digital media, and thus can find it difficult to form connections in their new country; others find themselves living without roots. The inhabitants of destination countries, too, find the welcoming of newcomers challenging. All experience the impact resulting from encountering diverse geographical, cultural and linguistic origins and are called to build intercultural communities. The impact of the phenomenon of migration on the life of the Church should not be overlooked. In this sense, the situation of some Eastern Catholic Churches is emblematic of this reality, with a growing number of faithful living in the diaspora. Maintaining links between those dispersed and their own Church of origin whilst creating new ones that respect diverse spiritual and cultural roots requires that new approaches be taken.

113. The spread of digital culture, particularly evident among young people, is profoundly changing their experience of space and time; it influences their daily activities, communication and interpersonal relationships, including faith. The opportunities that the internet provides are reshaping relationships, bonds and boundaries. Nowadays, we often experience loneliness and marginalisation, even though we are more connected than ever. Moreover, those with their own economic and political interests can exploit social media to spread ideologies and generate aggressive and manipulative forms of polarisation. We are not well prepared for this and ought to dedicate resources to ensure that the digital environment becomes a prophetic space for mission and proclamation. Local Churches should encourage, sustain and accompany those who are engaged in mission in the digital environment. Christian digital communities and groups, particularly young people, are also called to reflect on how they create bonds of belonging, promoting encounter and dialogue. They need to offer formation among their peers, developing a synodal way of being Church. The internet, constituted as a web of connections, offers new opportunities better to live the synodal dimension of the Church.

114. These social and cultural developments challenge the Church to reconsider the meaning of 'local' in its life and to review its organisational structures so that they can better serve its mission. It is essential to understand 'place' as the real and actual setting in which we come to experience our humanity, without denying that there is a geographical and cultural dimension to this as well. Here, where the web of relationships is established, the Church is called to express its sacramentality (cf. LG 1) and to carry out its mission.

115. The relation between place and space leads us also to reflect on the Church as 'home'. When it is not thought of as a closed space, inaccessible, to be defended at all costs, the image of home evokes the possibility of welcome, hospitality, and inclusion. Creation itself is our common home, where members of the one human family live with all other creatures. Our commitment, supported by the Spirit, is to ensure that the Church is perceived as a welcoming home, a sacrament of encounter and salvation, a school of communion for all the sons and daughters of God. The Church is also the People of God walking with Christ, in it everyone is called to be a pilgrim of hope. The traditional practice of pilgrimage is a sign of this. Popular piety is one of the places of a missionary synodal Church.

116. The local Church, understood as a diocese or eparchy, is the fundamental sphere in which the communion in Christ of the Baptised is most fully manifested. As local Church, the community is gathered in the celebration of the Eucharist presided over by its Bishop. Each local Church has its own internal organisation, whilst also maintaining relationships with other local Churches.

117. The parish is one of the main organising units in the local Church present throughout our history. The parish community that gathers in the celebration of the Eucharist is a privileged place of relationships, welcome, discernment and mission. Changes in how we experience and live our relationship with locality require us to reconsider how parishes are configured. What characterises

the parish is that it is a community that is not self-selecting. People gather there from different generations, professions, geographical origins and social classes and status. Responding to the new needs of mission requires opening up to new forms of pastoral action that take into account the mobility of people and the space in which their life unfolds. By placing a special emphasis on Christian initiation and offering accompaniment and formation, the parish community will be able to support people in the different stages of life in fulfilling their mission in the world. In this way, it will become more evident that the parish is not centred on itself but oriented towards mission. The parish is then called to sustain the commitment of so many people who in so many ways live and bear witness to their faith in through their profession, in social, cultural and political activities. In many regions of the world, small Christian communities or basic ecclesial communities are the terrain where meaningful relationships of closeness and reciprocity can flourish, offering the opportunity to experience synodality concretely.

118. We recognise that institutes of consecrated life, societies of apostolic life, as well as associations, movements and new communities, have the ability to take root locally and, at the same time, connect different places and milieus, often at a national or international level. Their action, together with that of many individuals and informal groups, often brings the Gospel to highly diverse contexts: to hospitals, prisons, homes for the elderly, reception centres for migrants, minors, those marginalised and victims of violence; to centres of education and training, schools and universities where young people and families meet; to the arenas of culture and politics and of integral human development, where new forms of living together are imagined and constructed. We look with gratitude also to monasteries, which are places of gathering and discernment and speak of a "beyond" that concerns the whole Church and directs its path. It is the particular responsibility of the Bishop or Eparch to animate these diverse bodies and to nurture the bonds of unity.

Institutes and associations are called to act in synergy with the local Church, participating in the dynamism of synodality.

119. Placing greater value on the 'intermediate' spaces between the local Church and the universal Church – such as ecclesiastical provinces and national and continental groupings of Churches – can foster a more meaningful presence of the Church in the world of today. Increased mobility and interconnectedness make the boundaries between Churches fluid, requiring ministry across a "great socio-cultural region". Such ministry needs to ensure that the Christian life "be adapted to the character and disposition of each culture" while avoiding all "false particularism" (AG 22).

## THE EXCHANGE OF GIFTS

120. Our walking together as disciples of Jesus in these different places, with our diverse charisms and ministries, while at the same time engaging in the exchange of gifts among the Churches, is an effective sign of the love and mercy of God in Christ breathed out in the Spirit who accompanies, sustains and directs humanity's journey towards the Reign of God. This exchange of gifts involves every aspect of Church life. The Church fulfils its mission by taking up and encouraging "the riches, resources and customs of peoples in so far as they are good; and in taking them up it purifies, strengthens and raises them up" (LG 13). It does so because it is both established in Christ as the People of God from all the peoples of the earth and is structured dynamically in a communion of local Churches, of their groupings, and of the Churches *sui iuris* within the one Catholic Church. The exhortation of the apostle Peter: "Like good stewards of the manifold grace of God, serve one another with whatever gift each of you has received" (*1 Pet* 4:10) can undoubtedly be applied to each local Church. The relationship between the Latin and the Eastern Catholic Churches is a paradigmatic and inspiring example of such an exchange of gifts. This relationship needs to be revivified and reconsidered with particular care due to changed and pressing historical circumstances. The exchange of

gifts and search for the common good within large transnational and intercultural geographical areas such as the Amazon, the Congo River basin, and the Mediterranean Sea is emerging as an example of newness and hope. This exchange includes a commitment to social issues of great global relevance.

121. The Church, both at the local level and by virtue of its Catholic unity, aspires to be a network of relationships which prophetically propagates and promotes a culture of encounter, social justice, inclusion of the marginalised, communion among peoples and care for the earth, our common home. The concrete realisation of this requires each Church to share its own resources in a spirit of solidarity, without paternalism or subordination, with respect for diversity and promoting healthy reciprocity. This includes, where necessary, a commitment to healing the wounds of memory and to walking the path of reconciliation. The exchange of gifts and the sharing of resources among local Churches belonging to different regions fosters the unity of the Church, creating bonds between the Christian communities involved. There is a need to focus on the conditions necessary to ensure that Priests who come to the aid of Churches needing clergy are not providing merely a functional solution but represent a resource for the growth both of the Church that sends them and the Church that receives them. Similarly, it is necessary to ensure that economic aid does not degenerate into the mere provision of welfare, but also promotes authentic evangelical solidarity and is managed transparently and reliably.

122. The exchange of gifts is of crucial significance in the journey towards full and visible unity among all Churches and Christian communions. Moreover, it represents an effective sign of the unity in the faith and love of Christ that promotes both the credibility and the impact of the Christian mission (cf. *Jn* 17:21). St John Paul II applied the following expression to ecumenical dialogue: "Dialogue is not simply an exchange of ideas. In some way it is always an 'exchange of gifts'". (UUS 28). Previous and ongoing efforts to incarnate the one Gospel by various Christian

traditions within a diversity of cultural contexts, historical circumstances and social challenges – attending to the Word of God and the voice of the Holy Spirit – have generated abundant fruit in holiness, charity, spirituality, theology, social and cultural solidarity. The time has come to treasure these precious riches: with generosity, sincerity, without prejudice, with gratitude to the Lord, and with mutual openness, gifting them to one another without assuming they are our exclusive property. The example of the saints and witnesses to the faith from other Christian Churches and Communions is also a gift that we can receive, including by inserting their memorial - especially that of the martyrs - into our liturgical calendar.

123. Pope Francis and the Grand Imam of Al-Azhar, Ahmed Al-Tayyeb, declared a commitment to adopt "a culture of dialogue as the path; mutual co-operation as the code of conduct; reciprocal understanding as the method and standard" in the *Document on Human Fraternity for World Peace and Living Together*, signed in Abu Dhabi on 4 February 2019. This is not an idle aspiration or something optional along the journey of the People of God in today's world. A synodal Church commits itself to walk this path alongside the believers of other religions and people of other beliefs wherever it lives. It freely shares the joy of the Gospel and gratefully receives their respective gifts. Through this collaboration, we aim to build together, as sisters and brothers, in a spirit of mutual activity and aid (cf. GS 40), justice, solidarity, peace and interreligious dialogue. In some regions, people meet in small neighbourhood communities irrespective of their religious belonging. These communities offer a favourable environment for a threefold dialogue: of life, of action and of prayer.

## THE BONDS OF UNITY: EPISCOPAL CONFERENCES AND ECCLESIAL ASSEMBLIES

124. The guiding principle of the relationship among Churches is the perspective of communion through the sharing of gifts.

This combines attention to the bonds that form the unity of the whole Church with the recognition and appreciation of the particularity of the context of each local Church, along with its history and tradition. A synodal style allows local Churches to move at different paces. Differences in pace can be valued as an expression of legitimate diversity and as an opportunity for sharing gifts and mutual enrichment. This common horizon requires discerning, identifying and promoting concrete practices which allow us to be a synodal Church on mission.

125. Episcopal Conferences express and implement the collegiality of the Bishops in order to foster communion between Churches and respond more effectively to the needs of pastoral life. They are a fundamental tool for creating bonds, sharing experiences and best practices among the Churches, and for adapting Christian life and the expression of faith to different cultures. With the involvement of the whole People of God, they also play an important role in the development of synodality. Based on the outcomes of the synodal process, we propose the following:

a) to gather the fruits of deliberations on the theological and juridical statute of Episcopal Conferences.

b) to specify precisely the domain of the doctrinal and disciplinary competence of Episcopal Conferences. Without compromising the authority of the Bishop within the Church entrusted to him or putting at risk either the unity or the catholicity of the Church, the collegial exercise of such competence can further the authentic teaching of the one faith in an appropriate and inculturated way within different contexts by identifying fitting liturgical, catechetical, disciplinary, pastoral theological and spiritual expression (cf. AG 22).

c) a process of evaluation of the experience of the concrete functioning of Episcopal Conferences, of the relations among the Bishops and with the Holy See so as to identify the particular reforms needed. The visits *ad limina Apostolorum* can provide appropriate occasions for this;

d) ensuring that all dioceses are part of an ecclesiastical province and of an Episcopal Conference;

e) specifying that decisions made by an Episcopal Conference impose an ecclesial obligation on each Bishop who participated in the decision in relation to his own diocese.

126. In the synodal process, the seven continental ecclesial assemblies that took place at the beginning of 2023 are both a relevant innovation and a legacy that we must treasure. They are an effective way of implementing conciliar teaching on the value of "each major socio-cultural area" in pursuit of "a more profound adaptation in the whole area of Christian life" (AG 22). In order to enable them to more fully contribute to the development of a synodal Church, it will be necessary to clarify the theological and canonical status of ecclesial assemblies, as well as that of the continental groupings of Episcopal Conferences. In particular, it is the responsibility of the Presidents of these groupings to encourage and sustain the continued development of this process.

127. In Ecclesial Assemblies (regional, national, continental) members who express and represent the diversity of the People of God (including Bishops) take part in the discernment that will enable Bishops, collegially, to reach decisions which it is proper for them to make by reason of their ministry. This experience demonstrates how synodality enables concretely the involvement of *all* (the holy People of God) and the ministry of *some* (the College of Bishops) in the decision-making process concerning the mission of the Church. We propose that discernment may include, in a manner appropriate to the diversity of contexts, spaces for listening and dialogue with other Christians and representatives of other religions, public institutions, civil society organisations and society at large.

128. In specific social and political circumstances, certain Episcopal Conferences face difficulties in participating in

continental assemblies or supranational ecclesial bodies. The Holy See has the responsibility to assist them by promoting dialogue and mutual trust with states, so that they may have the opportunity to engage with other Episcopal Conferences so that there may be the sharing of gifts.

129. To realise a "sound 'decentralization'" (EG 16) and an effective inculturation of faith, it is necessary not only to recognise the role of Episcopal Conferences, but also to rediscovery the institution of particular councils, both provincial and plenary. The periodic celebration of these councils was an obligation for much of the Church's history and is currently provided for in the canon law of the Latin Church (cf. CIC cann. 439-446). They should be convened periodically. The procedure for the recognition of the conclusions of particular councils by the Holy See (*recognitio*) should be reformed to encourage their timely publication by specifying precise deadlines or, in cases of purely pastoral or disciplinary matters (not directly concerning issues of faith, morals, or sacramental discipline), by introducing a legal presumption equivalent to tacit consent.

## THE SERVICE OF THE BISHOP OF ROME

130. The synodal process has also revisited the question of the ways in which the Bishop of Rome exercises his ministry. Synodality articulates in a symphonic manner the communitarian (all), collegial (some) and personal (one) dimensions of each local Church and of the whole Church. In the light of this, the Petrine ministry is inherent in the synodal dynamic, as is the communitarian dimension that includes the whole People of God, and the collegial one of the episcopal ministry (cf. ITC 64).

131. We can, therefore, understand the extent of the Council's affirmation that "within the ecclesiastical communion, there are lawfully particular Churches which enjoy their own proper traditions, while the primacy of the see of Peter remains intact, which presides over the universal communion of charity and safeguards legitimate differences while taking care that what is

particular not only does no harm to unity but rather is conducive to it" (LG 13). The Bishop of Rome, who is the foundation of the Church's unity (cf. LG 23), is the guarantor of synodality: he is the one who convokes the Church in Synod and presides over it, confirming its results. As the Successor of Peter, he has a unique role in safeguarding the deposit of faith and of morals, ensuring that synodal processes are geared towards unity and witness. Together with the Bishop of Rome, the College of Bishops has an irreplaceable role in shepherding the whole Church (cf. LG 22-23) and in promoting synodality in all the local Churches.

132. As guarantor of unity in diversity, the Bishop of Rome ensures that the identity of the Eastern Catholic Churches is safeguarded and that their centuries-old theological, canonical, liturgical, spiritual and pastoral traditions are respected. These Churches are equipped with their own deliberative synodal structures: Synod of Bishops of the Patriarchal Church, Synod of the Major Archepiscopal Church (cf. CCEO cann. 102 ss., 152), Provincial Council (cf. CCEO can. 137), Council of Hierarchs (cf. CCEO cann. 155, § 1, 164 ss.), and, lastly, Assemblies of Hierarchs of the various Churches *sui iuris* (cf. CCEO can. 322). As Churches *sui iuris* that are in full communion with the Bishop of Rome, they hold fast to their Eastern identity and their autonomy. In the framework of synodality, it is appropriate to revisit history together in order to heal the wounds of the past and to deepen how we live communion. This means giving consideration to adjusting relationships among Eastern Catholic Churches and the Roman Curia. Relationships among the Latin Church and Eastern Catholic Churches must be characterised by the exchange of gifts, collaboration and mutual enrichment.

133. In order to further these relations, the Synodal Assembly proposes to establish a Council of Patriarchs, Major Archbishops and Metropolitans of the Eastern Catholic Churches presided over by the Pope, which would be an expression of synodality and an instrument for promoting communion. The Council would also serve as a means of sharing liturgical, theological, canonical

and spiritual patrimony. The migration of many of the Eastern faithful into regions of the Latin Rite risks compromising their identity. Instruments and norms need to be evolved to strengthen as much as possible collaboration between the Latin Church and the Eastern Catholic Churches to address this situation. The Synodal Assembly recommends sincere dialogue and fraternal collaboration between Latin and Eastern Bishops, to ensure better pastoral care for the Eastern Faithful who lack Priests of their own rite and to guarantee, with the appropriate autonomy, the involvement of Eastern Bishops in Episcopal Conferences. Finally, the Assembly proposes that the Holy Father convene a Special Synod to promote the consolidation and re-flourishing of the Eastern Catholic Churches.

134. A synodal reflection on the exercise of the Petrine ministry must be undertaken from the perspective of the "sound 'decentralization'" (EG 16) wanted by Pope Francis and many Episcopal Conferences. According to the Apostolic Constitution *Prædicate Evangelium,* this decentralisation means "to leave to the competence of Bishops the authority to resolve, in the exercise of 'their proper task as teachers' and pastors, those issues with which they are familiar and that do not affect the Church's unity of doctrine, discipline and communion, always acting with that spirit of co-responsibility which is the fruit and expression of the specific *mysterium communionis* that is the Church" (PE II, 2). To keep progressing in this direction, one could initiate a theological and canonical study whose task would be to identify those matters that should be addressed to the Pope (*reservatio papalis*) and those that could be addressed to the Bishops in their Churches or groupings of Churches. This should be done in line with the recent Motu Proprio *Competentias quasdam decernere* (February 15, 2022). The document assigns "certain areas of competence with regard to the provisions of the Codes intended to safeguard unity of discipline in the universal Church, and executive power in the local Churches and ecclesial institutions" on the basis of "the dynamic of ecclesiastical communion"

(Preamble). Even canonical norms should be developed in a synodal style by those who have the relevant responsibility and authority and should be allowed to ripen as the fruit of ecclesial discernment.

135. The Apostolic Constitution *Prædicate Evangelium* has configured the service of the Roman Curia in a synodal and missionary sense. It insists that it "is not set between the Pope and the Bishops, but is at the service of both, according to the modalities proper to the nature of each" (PE I, 8). Its implementation ought to promote greater collaboration among the dicasteries and encourage their listening to local Churches. Before publishing important normative documents, the dicasteries are exhorted to initiate a consultation with Episcopal Conferences and with the corresponding structures of the Eastern Catholic Churches. In accordance with the rationale of transparency and accountability outlined above, forms of evaluating the work of the Curia might possibly be envisaged. Such an evaluation, in a synodal and missionary perspective, could also be extended to the Pontifical Representatives. The visits *ad limina Apostolorum* are the apex of the relation between the Bishops of local Churches and the Bishop of Rome and his closest collaborators in the Roman Curia. Many Bishops desire that the way these visits are conducted will be reviewed to make them more and more an opportunity for open exchange and mutual listening. Considering their diverse cultures and backgrounds, it is important, for the good of the Church, that members of the College of Cardinals become better acquainted with one another and that the bonds of communion among them be fostered. Synodality should inspire their collaboration with the Petrine Ministry and their collegial discernment in ordinary and extraordinary consistories.

136. The Synod of Bishops emerges as one of the most evident places where synodality and collegiality are to be practised. The Apostolic Constitution *Episcopalis communio* has transformed this from an event to an ecclesial process. The Synod was

established by St Paul VI as an assembly of Bishops convoked to support the Roman Pontiff in his concern for the whole Church. Today, transformed into a phased process, it fosters the essential relationship between the People of God, the College of Bishops and the Pope. The whole holy People of God, the Bishops to whom portions of the People of God are entrusted, and the Bishop of Rome participate fully in the synodal process, each according to their proper function. This participation is made manifest in the varied composition of the Synodal Assembly gathered around the Pope, which reflects the catholicity of the Church. In particular, as Pope Francis explained, the composition of this XVI Ordinary General Assembly is "more than a contingent fact. It expresses a way of exercising the episcopal ministry consistent with the living Tradition of the Churches and with the teaching of Second Vatican Council" (*Address to the First General Congregation of the Second Session of the XVI General Ordinary Assembly of the Synod of Bishops*, 2 October 2024). The Synod of Bishops, preserving its episcopal nature, has seen and will be able to see in the future in the participation of other members of the People of God "the form that the exercise of episcopal authority is called to take in a Church that is conscious of being essentially relational and therefore synodal" (*ibid.*) for mission. In deepening the identity of the Synod of Bishops, what is essential is that the combination of the involvement of *all* (the holy People of God), the ministry of *some* (the College of Bishops) and the presidency of *one* (the successor of Peter) appears and is concretely realised throughout the synodal process and in the Assemblies.

137. One of the most significant fruits of the Synod 2021-2024 has been the intensity of ecumenical zeal. The need to find "a way of exercising the primacy which [...] is nonetheless open to a new situation" (UUS 95) is a fundamental challenge both for a missionary synodal Church and for Christian unity. The Synod welcomes the recent publication of the Dicastery for Promoting Christian Unity *The Bishop of Rome: Primacy and Synodality in Ecumenical Dialogues and in the Responses to the Encyclical Ut*

*Unum Sint,* which opens avenues for further study. The document shows that the promotion of Christian unity is an essential aspect of the ministry of the Bishop of Rome and that the ecumenical journey has fostered a deeper understanding of it. The concrete proposals it contains regarding a re-reading or an official commentary on the dogmatic definitions of the First Vatican Council on primacy, a clearer distinction between the different responsibilities of the Pope, the promotion of synodality within the Church and in its relationship with the world and the search for a model of unity based on an ecclesiology of communion offer promising prospects for the ecumenical journey. The Synodal Assembly hopes that this document will serve as a basis for further reflection with other Christians, "together, of course", on the exercise of the Ministry of Unity of the Bishop of Rome as a "service of love recognised by all concerned" (UUS 95).

138. The richness of the participation of Fraternal Delegates from other Churches and Christian Communions at the synodal Assembly invites us to pay more attention to the synodal practices of our ecumenical partners, both in the East and in the West. Ecumenical dialogue is fundamental to developing an understanding of synodality and the unity of the Church. It urges us to develop ecumenical synodal practices, including forms of consultation and discernment on questions of shared and urgent interest, as the celebration of an ecumenical Synod on evangelisation could be. It also invites us to mutual accountability for who we are, what we do, and what we teach. What makes this possible is our unity under the one Baptism that offers us the dynamism of communion, participation and mission and which gives life to our identity as the People of God.

139. In 2025, the Year of Jubilee, we will also celebrate the anniversary of the Council of Nicaea, the First Ecumenical Council at which the symbol of the faith that unites all Christians was formulated. The preparation and joint commemoration of the 1700th anniversary of this event should be an opportunity to deepen and confess together our faith in Christ and to put into

practice forms of synodality among Christians of all traditions. It will also be an opportunity to launch bold initiatives for a common date for Easter so that we can celebrate the Resurrection of the Lord on the same day, as will happen, providentially, in 2025. This will give greater missionary strength to the proclamation of Him, who is the life and salvation of the whole world.

# PART V - "SO I SEND YOU"

# FORMING A PEOPLE FOR MISSIONARY DISCIPLESHIP

*Jesus said to them again, "Peace be with you. As the Father has sent me, so I send you." When he had said this, he breathed on them and said to them, "Receive the Holy Spirit."* (Jn *20, 21-22*).

140. On the evening of the Resurrection, Jesus gave the disciples the salvific gift of His peace and made them sharers in His mission. His peace represents the fullness of life, harmony with God, with sisters and brothers, and with creation. His mission is to proclaim the Reign of God, offering to every person, without exception, the mercy and love of the Father. The subtle gesture that accompanies the words of the Risen One recalls what God did in the beginning. Now, in the Upper Room, with the breath of the Spirit, the new creation begins: a People of missionary disciples is born.

141. The holy People of God require proper formation so that they can witness to the joy of the Gospel and grow in the practice of synodality: first of all, in the freedom of sons and daughters of God in following Jesus Christ, contemplated in prayer and recognised in those who are poor. Synodality implies a profound vocational and missionary awareness, the source of a renewed way of living ecclesial relations and new dynamics regarding participation. It also means adopting the practice of ecclesial discernment and a culture of ongoing evaluation. These cannot come about unless accompanied by focused formation processes. Formation in synodality and the Church's synodal style will make people aware that the gifts received in Baptism should be put to use for the good of all: they cannot be hidden or remain unused.

142. The formation of missionary disciples begins with and is rooted in Christian Initiation. In each person's journey of faith, there is an encounter with many people, groups and small communities that have helped foster their relationship with the Lord and introduce them in the communion of the Church: parents and family members, godparents, catechists and educators, liturgical leaders and those providing charitable services, Deacons, Priests and the Bishop himself. Sometimes, once the journey of Initiation is over, the bond with the community weakens, and formation becomes neglected. However, becoming missionary disciples of the Lord is not something achieved once and for all. It demands continuous conversion, growing in love "to the measure of the full stature of Christ" (*Eph* 4:13) and being open to the gifts of the Spirit for a living and joyful witness of faith. This is why it is important to rediscover how the Sunday Eucharist is formative for Christians: "The full extent of our formation is our conformation to Christ [...]: it does not have to do with an abstract mental process, but with becoming Him" (DD 41). For many of the faithful, the Sunday Eucharist is their only contact with the Church: ensuring it is celebrated in the best possible manner, with particular regard to the homily and to the "active participation" (SC 14) of everyone, is decisive for synodality. In the Mass, we experience synodality coming to life in the Church as a grace received from above. This precedes the synodality that comes about as the result of our own efforts. Under the presidency of *one* and thanks to the ministry of *a few*, *all* can participate at the twofold table of the Word and the Bread. The gift of communion, mission and participation - the three cornerstones of synodality - is realised and renewed in every Eucharist.

143. One of the requests that emerged most strongly and from all contexts during the synodal process is that the formation provided by the Christian community be integral, ongoing and shared. Such formation must aim not only at acquiring theoretical knowledge but also at promoting the capacity for

openness and encounter, sharing and collaboration, reflection and discernment in common. Formation must consequently engage all the dimensions of the human person (intellectual, affective, relational and spiritual) and include concrete experiences that are appropriately accompanied. There was also a marked insistence throughout the synodal process upon the need for a common and shared formation, in which men and women, laity, consecrated persons, ordained ministers and candidates for ordained ministry participate together, thus enabling them to grow together in knowledge and mutual esteem and in the ability to collaborate. This requires the presence of suitable and competent formators, capable of demonstrating with their lives what they transmit with their words. Only in this way will formation be truly generative and transformative. Nor should we overlook the contribution that the pedagogical disciplines can make to providing well-focused formation, adult learning and teaching methods and the accompaniment of individuals and communities. We, therefore, need to invest in the formation of formators.

144. The Church already has many places and resources for the formation of missionary disciples: families, small communities, parishes, ecclesial associations, seminaries and religious communities, academic institutions, and also places for serving and working with the marginalised, as well as missionary and volunteer initiatives. In each of these areas, the community expresses its capacity to educate in discipleship and to accompany through witness. This encounter often brings together people of different generations, from the youngest to the oldest. In the Church, no one simply receives formation: everyone is an active subject and has something to give to others. Popular piety, too, is a precious treasure of the Church, which teaches the whole People of God on the journey.

145. Among the formative practices that can benefit from the new impetus of synodality, special attention should be given to catechesis so that, in addition to being part of the journey of

initiation, catechesis is continuously drawing people outwards in mission. Communities of missionary disciples will know how to implement catechesis under the sign of mercy and bring it closer to each person's lived experience, taking it to the existential peripheries without losing the *Catechism of the Catholic Church* as a reference point. It can thus become a 'laboratory of dialogue' with the men and women of our time (cf. Pontifical Council for Promoting New Evangelisation, *Directory for Catechesis*, 54) and illuminate their search for meaning. In many Churches, catechists are the fundamental resource for accompaniment and formation; in others, their service must be better appreciated and supported by the community, breaking away from a logic of delegation, which contradicts synodality. Taking into account the scale of the phenomena of human migration, it is important that catechesis promotes deeper relationships of mutual acquaintance amongst Churches of origin and destination.

146. In addition to specifically pastoral settings and resources, the Christian community is present in many other places of formation, such as in schools, vocational training colleges, and universities, as well as where people are formed for social and political commitment and in the worlds of sport, music and art. Despite the diversity of cultural contexts, which determine very different practices and traditions, Catholic-inspired formation centres are increasingly finding themselves on the frontline of a Church that is always moving outwards in mission. Inspired by the practices of synodality, they can become fertile contexts for friendly and participative relationships. They become contexts that give witness to life; in them, the skills and organisation are, above all, lay-led, and the contribution of families is prioritised. In particular, Catholic schools and universities play an important role in the dialogue between faith and culture and in providing moral education on values, offering a formation oriented towards Christ, the icon of life in its fullness. Thus, they become capable of promoting an alternative to the dominant models that are often driven by individualism and competition, thereby also playing

a prophetic role. In some contexts, they are the only settings where children and young people come into contact with the Church. When inspired by intercultural and interreligious dialogue, their educational engagement is also valued by those of other religious traditions as a form of human development.

147. Shared synodal formation for all the Baptised constitutes the horizon within which to understand and practise the specific formation required for individual ministries and vocations. For this to happen, it must be implemented as an exchange of gifts between different vocations (communion), in the perspective of a service to be performed (mission) and in a style of involvement and education in differentiated co-responsibility (participation). This request, which emerged strongly from the synodal process, often requires a demanding change of mentality and a renewed approach to both formation contexts and processes. Above all, it implies an inner readiness to be enriched by the encounter with brothers and sisters in the faith, overcoming prejudices and partisan views. The ecumenical dimension of formation cannot but facilitate this change in mentality.

148. Throughout the synodal process, a widely expressed request was that the discernment and formation of candidates for ordained ministry be undertaken in a synodal way. There should be a significant presence of women, an immersion in the daily life of communities, and formation to enable collaboration with everyone in the Church and in how to practise ecclesial discernment. This implies a courageous investment of energy in the preparation of formators. The Assembly calls for a revision of the *Ratio Fundamentalis Institutionis Sacerdotalis* in order to incorporate the requests made by the Synod. They should be translated into precise guidelines for a formation to synodality. Formation pathways should awaken in candidates their passion for the mission to all peoples (*ad gentes*). Formation of Bishops is just as necessary so that they may better assume their mission of bringing together in unity the gifts of the Spirit and exercise in a synodal manner the authority conferred on them. The synodal

way of formation implies that the ecumenical dimension is present in all aspects of the paths towards ordained ministries.

149. The synodal process has insistently drawn attention to some specific areas of formation of the People of God for synodality. The first of these concerns the impact of the digital environment on learning processes, concentration, the perception of self and the world, and the building of interpersonal relationships. Digital culture constitutes a crucial dimension of the Church's witness in contemporary culture and an emerging missionary field. This requires ensuring that the Christian message is present online in reliable ways that do not ideologically distort its content. Although digital media has great potential to improve our lives, it can also cause harm and injury through bullying, misinformation, sexual exploitation and addiction. Church educational institutions must help children and adults develop critical skills safely to navigate the web.

150. Another area of great importance is the promotion in all ecclesial contexts of a culture of safeguarding, making communities ever safer places for minors and vulnerable persons. The work to equip Church structures with regulations and legal procedures that enable the prevention of abuse and timely responses to inappropriate behaviour has already begun. It is necessary to continue this commitment, offering ongoing specific and adequate formation to those who work in contact with minors and vulnerable adults so that they can act competently and recognise the signals, often silent, of those experiencing difficulties and needing help. It is essential that victims are welcomed and supported, and this needs to be done sensitively. This requires great humanity and must be carried out with the help of qualified people. We must all allow ourselves to be moved by their suffering and practise that proximity, which, through concrete choices, will uplift them, help them and prepare a different future for all. Safeguarding processes must be constantly monitored and evaluated. Victims and survivors must be welcomed and supported with great sensitivity.

151. The concerns of the Church's social doctrine, commitment to peace and justice, care for our common home and intercultural and interreligious dialogue, must also be more widely shared among the People of God so that the action of missionary disciples can influence the construction of a more just and compassionate world. The commitment to defending life and human rights, for the proper ordering of society, for the dignity of work, for a fair and supportive economy, and an integral ecology is part of the evangelising mission that the Church is called to live and incarnate in history.

# CONCLUSION

# A FEAST FOR ALL PEOPLES

*When they had gone ashore, they saw a charcoal fire there, with fish on it, and bread. [...] Jesus said to them, "Come and have breakfast". Now none of the disciples dared to ask him, "Who are you?" because they knew it was the Lord. Jesus came and took the bread and gave it to them, and did the same with the fish.* (*Jn 21, 9.12.13*).

152. The miraculous catch of fish concludes with a feast. The Risen One asked the disciples to obey His Word, to cast their nets and pull them ashore. It is He, however, who prepares the banquet and invites them to eat. There are loaves and fish for all, just as when He multiplied them for the hungry crowd. Most of all, there is the wonder and enchantment of His presence, so clear and bright that no one needs to ask questions. Eating with them once again, following their abandonment and denial of Him, He invites them anew into communion with Him, imprinting upon them the sign of His eternal mercy that opens onto the future. Those who participated in this Easter would thus identify themselves as those "who ate and drank with him after he rose from the dead." (*Acts* 10:41).

153. By sharing meals with His disciples, the Risen Lord fulfils the image of the prophet Isaiah, whose words have inspired the work of the Synodal Assembly: a superabundant and sumptuous banquet prepared by the Lord on the mountaintop, a symbol of conviviality and communion intended for all peoples (cf. *Is* 25:6-8). The breakfast that the Lord prepared for His disciples after Easter is a sign that the eschatological banquet had already begun. Even if it finds its fullness only in Heaven, the banquet of grace and mercy is already prepared for all. The Church has the

mission of bringing this splendid announcement to a changing world. While nourished in the Eucharist by the Lord's Body and Blood, the Church is aware it cannot forget the poorest, the last, the excluded, those who do not know love and are without hope, nor those who do not believe in God or do not recognise themselves in any established religion. In its prayer, the Church brings them to the Lord and then goes out to meet them with the creativity and boldness that the Spirit inspires. The Church's synodality thus becomes a social prophecy for today's world, inspiring new paths in the political and economic spheres, as well as collaborating with all those who believe in fellowship and peace in an exchange of gifts with the world.

154. Living through the synodal process, we have renewed our awareness that the salvation to be received and proclaimed is inherently relational. We live it and witness to it together. History reveals itself to us tragically marked by war, rivalry for power and thousands of injustices and abuses. We know, however, that the Spirit has placed the desire for authentic relationships and true bonds in the heart of every human being. Creation itself speaks of unity and sharing, of diversity and of variously interconnected forms of life. Everything stems from and tends towards harmony, even while being devastated by evil. The ultimate meaning of synodality is the witness that the Church is called to give to God, Father, Son and Holy Spirit, the harmony of love that pours Himself out, to give Himself to the world. We can live the communion that saves by walking in a synodal way, in the intertwining of our vocations, charisms and ministries, by going forth to meet everyone in order to bring the joy of the Gospel: communion with God, with the entire humanity and all of creation. In this way, thanks to this sharing, we have already begun to experience the banquet of life that God offers to all peoples.

155. We entrust the results of this Synod to the Virgin Mary, who bears the splendid title of *Odigitria*, she who shows and guides the way. May she, Mother of the Church, who in the

Upper Room helped the newly formed community of disciples to open themselves to the novelty of Pentecost, teach us to be a People of disciples and missionaries walking together, to be a synodal Church.

*Vatican, 26 October 2024*

Franciscus

# APPENDIX

The texts of the Holy Father contained in the Appendix refer to the Second Session of the XVI Ordinary General Assembly of the Synod of Bishops (2-27 October 2024).

## 1ST GENERAL CONGREGATION
## OPENING ADDRESS

Paul VI Hall, Wednesday 2 October 2024

*Dear Brothers and Sisters,*

Since the Church of God was "convened in Synod" in October 2021, we have all travelled along part of the long journey to which God the Father has always called His people. He invites them to bring to all nations the good news that Jesus Christ is our peace (*Eph* 2,14) and confirms them with the Holy Spirit in their mission.

This Assembly, guided by the Holy Spirit, who "bends the stubborn heart and will, melts the frozen, warms the chill, guides the steps that go astray" (*Pentecost Sequence*), will need Him to make His contribution for there to be a Synodal, missionary Church, which can move outwards and settle in the geographical and existential outskirts, making every effort to establish links with everyone there, in Christ our Brother and Lord.

There is a text by a fourth century spiritual author, which sums up what happens when the Holy Spirit gets to work at Baptism, which grants equal dignity to all (cf. Macarius of Alexandria, *Hom* 18, 7-11: PG 34, 639-642). The experiences Macarius describes help us to recognise how much has happened in the past three years, and how much is yet to happen.

This spiritual author's reflection helps us to understand that the Holy Spirit is a trusty guide, and our first task is to learn to distinguish his voice, because He speaks in everyone and in all things. The synodal experience has allowed us to experience this.

The Holy Spirit always accompanies us. The Spirit consoles us in moments of sorrow and grief, especially when – precisely because of our love of humanity – we confront things that are not going well, injustices that seem to prevail, resistances to respond to evil with good, difficulties in forgiving; lack of courage in seeking peace. In these moments it seems that there is nothing more to do and we are gripped by despair. Just as hope is the humblest yet the strongest virtue, despair is the worst.

The Holy Spirit dries our tears and consoles us because He imparts God's hope. God is tireless, because His love is tireless.

The Holy Spirit penetrates into that part of us which is often just like a court of law, where we put the accused in the witness-box and make our judgements, usually finding them guilty. Macarius himself, in his homily, tells us that the Holy Spirit kindles, in those who receive him, a fire, a "fire of such joy and love that, were it possible, all without discrimination, bad and good alike, would take into their own hearts". This is because God accepts everyone, always; let us not forget: everyone, everyone, everyone, and always; and he offers them all new possibilities in life, right up to the last moment. That is why we must forgive everyone, always, aware that the willingness to forgive comes from the experience of having been forgiven. Only one is unable to forgive: the one who has not been forgiven.

Yesterday, during the penitential vigil, we had that experience. We asked pardon, and we recognised that we are sinners. We put pride on one aside and cut ourselves off from presuming that we are better than others. Did we become any humbler?

Humility, too, is the Holy Spirit's gift: we should ask for it. As the etymology of the word tells us, humility brings us back down to earth, to the *humus*, and it reminds us of our origin, when, without the Creator's breath, we would still have been lifeless mud. Humility lets us look at the world and admit we are no better than anyone else. As St Paul says: "do not be wise in your own estimation" (*Rom* 12,16). And one cannot be humble without love. Christians should be like those women Dante Alighieri described in a sonnet, women with sorrow in their hearts for the loss of their friend Beatrice's father: "You who bear a humble look, with eyes cast down, displaying sadness" (*Vita Nuova* XXII, 9). This is the humility of solidarity and compassion, the humility of those who feel like a brother or sister to everyone else; they suffer their pain and recognise, in their wounds and sufferings, the wounds and sufferings of Our Lord.

I encourage you to meditate in prayer on this fine spiritual text and to recognise that the Church - *semper reformanda* - cannot continue on her journey and be renewed without the Holy Spirit and His surprises; without allowing herself to be formed, by the hands of God the Creator, by the Son, Jesus Christ, and by the Holy Spirit, as St Irenæus of Lyons teaches us (cf. *Adv. Hær.* IV, 20, 1).

Ever since God, in the beginning, created man and woman from the earth; ever since God called Abraham to be a blessing for all the peoples of the earth and called Moses to lead across the desert a people freed from slavery; ever since the Virgin Mary welcomed the Word which made her the Mother of God's Son according to the flesh, and the Mother of all the men and women who would become her Son's disciples; ever since the crucified and risen Lord Jesus poured out his Holy Spirit at Pentecost: ever since then, we have been travelling, as those who have been "shown mercy", towards the total, definitive fulfilment of the Father's love. And let us not forget that: we have been "shown mercy".

We know how beautiful and tiring that journey has been. We are making it together as a people who, even in our own day, are a sign and an instrument of intimate union with God and of the unity of the whole human race (cf. LG 1). We are making it with and for every man and woman of good will, in each of whom grace is invisibly working (cf. GS 22). We are making it, convinced of the "relational" nature of the Church and taking care that the relationships given to us and entrusted to our responsibility and creativity will always be a sign that mercy is freely available. A so-called Christian who does not enter into God's gratuitousness and mercy is simply an atheist disguised as a Christian. God's mercy makes us trustworthy and responsible.

Sisters, brothers, let us make this journey, mindful that we have been called to reflect the light of our sun, who is Christ, like a pale moon which faithfully and joyously takes on the mission of being for the world a sacrament of that light, a light that does not shine out of us.

The XVI General Ordinary Assembly of the Synod of Bishops, which has now reached its Second Session, represents this common journey of the People of God in a novel way.

The inspiration which came to Pope St Paul VI, when he instituted the Synod of Bishops in 1965, has proved quite fruitful. In the intervening sixty years, we have learnt to recognise the Synod of Bishops as a plural and symphonic subject which is capable of sustaining the Catholic Church's journey and mission, an effective help for the Bishop of Rome in his service to the communion of all the Churches and of the whole Church.

St Paul VI was quite aware that "this Synod, [...] like all human institutions, can be improved upon with the passing of time" (*Apostolica Sollicitudo*). The Apostolic Constitution *Episcopalis communio* was meant to build on the experience of the various synodal Assemblies (Ordinary, Extraordinary and Special) and to present the synodal Assembly explicitly as a process and not only as an event.

The synodal process is also a learning process, in the course of which the Church gets to know herself better and to identify the most suitable forms of pastoral action for the mission her Lord entrusts to her. The learning process also involves the ways pastors, and particularly Bishops, exercise their ministry.

When I decided to convene also – as full members of this XVI Assembly – a significant number of Lay and Consecrated people (men and women), Deacons and Priests, developing what somehow had already been envisaged for earlier Assemblies,

I did so in accordance with the Second Vatican Ecumenical Council's understanding of the ministry of bishops: the Bishop, the principle and visible basis of unity of each particular Church, cannot live out his service except within the People of God, with the People of God, leading, standing among, and following the portion of the People of God that has been entrusted to him. The manifestation and identification of this inclusive understanding of episcopal ministry needs to avoid two dangers: first, an abstract approach which ignores the fertile concreteness of places and relationships and the value of each individual; second, pitting hierarchy and faithful against each other in a way that fractures communion. It is certainly not a question of replacing one with the other, urged on by cries like: "now it's our turn"! No, this is not right: "now it's up to us laypeople", "now it's up to us priests". No. This is not right. On the contrary, what we are asked to do is to operate together in a symphonic style, in a composition that unites us all at the service of God's mercy, according to the different ministries and charisms that the Bishop has the task of recognising and promoting.

Journeying together with everyone – everyone, everyone together – is a process in which the Church, submitting to the action of the Holy Spirit, and sensitive enough to capture the signs of the times (cf. GS 4), continually renews herself and perfects her sacramental nature, in order to be a credible witness of the mission to which she is called, to unite all peoples into the one people awaited at the end, when God Himself will ask us to be seated at the banquet prepared by Him (*cf. Is* 25,6-10).

The composition of this XVI Assembly is thus more than a contingent fact. It expresses a way of exercising episcopal ministry which is consistent with the living Tradition of the Churches and with the teaching of the Second Vatican Council: never should a Bishop, or any other Christian, think of himself "without others". Just as nobody is saved alone, the proclamation of salvation requires everyone, and demands that everyone be heard.

The presence at the Assembly of the Synod of Bishops of non-episcopal members does not diminish the "episcopal" character of the Assembly. Still less does it place some limit on or derogate from the authority of individual Bishops or of the episcopal College (I say this because of some sort of rumpus caused by gossips running around all over the place). Rather, it indicates the form the exercise of episcopal authority is called to have in a Church which is aware of being constitutively relational and thus synodal. The relationship with Christ and with others in Christ – those who are there and those who are not yet there, but are awaited by the Father – completes the substance and moulds the shape of the whole Church at all times.

Different "collegial" and "synodal" forms of exercising episcopal ministry (in particular Churches, in groupings of Churches, in the Church as a whole) will need to be identified in due course, always with respect for the deposit of faith and living Tradition, always in response to what the Holy Spirit is asking of the Churches at this particular time and in the various contexts in which they live. And let us not forget that the Spirit is harmony. Let us think of the morning of Pentecost: there was fearful disorder, but He brought harmony in that disorder. Let us not forget that He really is harmony. It is not a sophisticated, intellectual harmony; it is everything, an existential harmony.

It is the Holy Spirit who makes the Church perennially faithful to the Lord Jesus Christ's command and attentive to His Word. The Spirit guides the disciples to the entire truth (Cf. *Jn* 16,13). He is guiding us, too, gathered in the Holy Spirit in this Assembly, to give an answer, after a journey of three years, to the question how to be a synodal Church in mission. I would add "merciful".

With a heart full of hope and gratitude, aware of the demanding task which has been given to you (and which has been given to *us*), I hope all will open themselves willingly to the action of the Holy Spirit, our trusty guide, our consolation. Thank you.

# 17TH GENERAL CONGREGATION FINAL GREETING

## Paul VI Hall, Saturday 26 October 2024

*Dear Brothers and Sisters,*

With the *Final Document*, we have gathered up the fruit of years – at least three – during which we set out to listen to the People of God, in order to have a better understanding, by listening to the Holy Spirit, of how to be a "synodal Church" in these times. The biblical references at the beginning of each chapter set out the message by linking it to the actions and words of our Risen Lord, who calls us to be witnesses of His Gospel, with our lives more than with our words.

The Document on which we have voted is a gift three times over.

1. First of all, it is a gift for me, the Bishop of Rome. When I convoked the Church of God in Synod, I was aware that I needed you, the Bishops and the witnesses of the synodal path. Thank you!

I often remind myself, and to you, that the Bishop of Rome, too, needs to practise listening; in fact, he wants to do it, in order to respond to the Word, which tells him every day: "Strengthen your brothers and sisters.... Feed my lambs".

You are well aware that my task is to protect and promote the harmony which – as St Basil teaches us – the Spirit continues to disseminate in God's Church, in the relations between the Churches, despite all the efforts, tensions and divisions that mark its journey towards the full manifestation of the Kingdom of God, which the Prophet Isaiah asks us to imagine as a banquet God will prepare for all peoples. All of them and everyone, in the hope that none will be missing. Everyone, everyone, everyone! Nobody left outside: everyone. And here is the key word: harmony. The first strong manifestation of what the Spirit does, on the morning of Pentecost, is to bring harmony among all our differences and all our languages... Harmony. It is what Vatican II teaches by saying that the Church is "like a sacrament": it is sign and instrument of God's anticipation; He has already set the table, and He waits expectantly. Through His Spirit, His grace whispers words of love in everyone's heart. It is up to us to amplify the sound of this whispering, never getting in its way; to open the doors, never building walls. How much damage the women and men of the Church do when they build walls, how much damage! Everyone is welcome, everyone, everyone! We must not behave like "dispensers of grace", who steal the treasure and tie the hands of our merciful God. Remember that we began this synodal Assembly by asking forgiveness, feeling shame and recognising that we are all beneficiaries of mercy.

There is a poem by Madeleine Delbrêl, the mystic of the peripheries, who urged: "Above all, do not be rigid" – rigidity is a sin, a sin which sometimes gets into the hearts of the clergy and of consecrated men and women. I'll read you some verses from Madeleine Delbrêl, which are in the form of a prayer. She says this:

*For I think that you may have had enough*
*of people who, always, speak of serving you with the look of a leader,*
*of encountering you with the air of a professor,*
*of approaching you with sporting regulations,*
*of loving you as one loves in an aged marriage.*
...
*Let us live our life,*
*not as a game of chess where everything is calculated,*
*not as a game where everything is difficult,*
*not as a theorem that breaks our minds,*
*but like an endless party where your meeting is renewed,*
*like a ball,*
*like a dance,*
*in the arms of your grace,*
*in the universal music of love.*

These verses can become the background music with which we receive the *Final Document*. And now, in the light of what has emerged from the synodal journey, there are and there will be decisions to be made.

In this time of wars, we must be witnesses of peace, and also learn to shape in concrete ways the *conviviality of differences*.

For this reason, I do not intend to publish an "Apostolic Exhortation": what we have approved is enough. The Document already contains very substantial indications which can guide the mission of the Churches, on different continents, and in particular contexts: hence I am making it available to everyone straight away; hence I have asked for it to be published. In this way, I want to acknowledge the value of the synodal journey which has been made, and which, by means of this Document, I entrust to the holy faithful People of God.

Time is needed in order to arrive at decisions and choices that involve the whole Church on some aspects of the life of the Church to which the Document draws attention, and on the themes entrusted to the ten "Study Groups", which need to work freely in order to offer me proposals. I shall, therefore, continue to listen to the Bishops and the Churches entrusted to them.

This is not the classic way of putting decisions off for ever. It is what corresponds to the synodal style with which the Petrine ministry, too, is to be exercised: listen, convene, discern, decide and evaluate. Pauses, silence and prayer are necessary at every one of these steps. It is a style we are learning together, a little at a time. The Holy Spirit calls us and supports us in this way of learning, which we need to see as a process of conversion.

The General Secretariat of the Synod and all the Dicasteries of the Roman Curia will help me in this task.

2. The Document is a gift to the whole faithful People of God, in all its various forms. It is obvious that not everyone will set about reading it: it will be you, above all, together with many

other people, who will make what it contains accessible in the local Churches. Without the witness of the experience acquired, the text would lose much of its value.

3. Dear brothers and sisters, what we have lived through is a gift we cannot keep to ourselves. The energy that comes from this experience, which is reflected in the Document, gives us the courage to bear witness that it is possible to walk together with our differences without condemning each other.

We come from all parts of the world, from places marked by violence, poverty and indifference. Together, with the hope that does not disappoint, united in the love of God which has been poured into our hearts, we can not only dream of peace, but commit ourselves with all our might so that, even if we don't say much about synodality, peace may be achieved through processes of listening, dialogue and reconciliation. The synodal Church for mission now needs the words we have shared to be backed up by deeds. And that is the path.

All of this is the Holy Spirit's gift: *it is He who creates harmony, He is harmony.* St Basil has a beautiful theology on this: if you can, read his treatise on the Holy Spirit. He is harmony. Brothers and sisters, may harmony continue even after we leave this Aula and may the breath of the Risen One help us to share the gifts we have received.

And remember – more words from Madeleine Delbrêl – that "there are places where the Spirit blows, but there is one Spirit who blows in every place".

I should like to thank you all; let us thank each other, too. I thank Cardinal Grech and Cardinal Hollerich for the work they have done, the two Under-Secretaries, Sister Becquart and Bishop Marín de San Martín – you've done well! – Father Battocchio and Father Costa, who have helped so much! I greet everyone who has worked behind the scenes; without them we would not have been able to do all this. Thank you so much! May the Lord bless you. Let us pray for each other. Thank you!